THE MAMMALIAN OF CHINA

Sheng Helin   Noriyuki Ohtaishi   Lu Houji

China Forestry Publishing House

图书在版编目（CIP）数据

中国野生哺乳动物：英文版/盛和林等编著．－北京：中国林业出版社，
1998.12
ISBN 7－5038－2072－1

I. 中… II. 盛… III. 哺乳动物纲－野生动物－简介－中国－英文
IV. Q959.808
中国版本图书馆 CIP 数据核字（98）第 23114 号

中国林业出版社出版
（100009　北京市西城区刘海胡同 7 号）
深圳新海彩印有限公司印刷
1999 年 3 月第 1 版　1999 年 3 月第 1 次印刷

Executive Editor：Li Wei，Chen Li
Book Design：Li Zhongxin

Printed in the People's Republic of China．
Archives Library of Chinese Publications Number 98 – 23114
International Standard Book Number 7 – 5038 – 2072 – 1

The Mammalian of China：Sheng Helin et al．， 1999
Incudes reference and index．
1．China… 2．Sheng… 3．The class of mammals-Wild animal-Introdution-China-English　4．Q959.808

China Forestry Publishing House
7， Liuhai Hutong， West City District，
Beijing， P.R． China， 100009
Tel：（010）66180373
Fax：（010）66180373
E-mail：cfphz@public.bta.net.cn

PREFACE

China is a large country boasting highly varied climatic, geographical, topographic and vegetative habitats supporting a great diversity of mammalian life. Five hundred thirty – four species of mammals under 14 orders and 56 families live in China, comprising about 12.5% of total living mammalian fauna on earth. China thus ranks among the most mammalian – diverse countries in the world.

Wild mammals are a vital component of the natural ecosystem and as such are indispensable to the well – being of mankind. Since the beginning of human history, man has exploited mammals for his own purposes, i. e. providing him with food, clothing, and medicine, as well as sport and recreation and even an outlet for human artistic expression. Today, mammals are exploited for the same purposes as in the past and will continue to be vitally important to man far into the future. In spite of their importance to man, however, more and more mammalian species in the world are in decline and/or in danger of extinction, often due to man – made problems. In China as everywhere, habitat destruction caused by human activity and population pressures, environmental pollution, pesticides, climatic change, etc. have caused severe depletion in numbers of many species, threatening the very survival of many of China's indigenous mammals. In the 1980s, the dwindling numbers of animals, especially among the medium – sized and large – sized mammals, set off an alarm in both the Chinese and international scientific communities. In an effort to check the rapid decline in wildlife within its borders, the Chinese Government enacted the *Wildlife Protection Law of the People's Republic of China* on November 8, 1988. In accordance with this Wildlife Protection Law, on December 10, 1988, the State Department issued a *Key List of Protected Animals* of all those wildlife species requiring governmental protection. Both the Wildlife Protection Law and the key List of Protected Animals have served as linchpins of official Chinese policy on domestic wildlife conservation issues ever since.

The purpose of Mammalian of China is multifold. It first aims to supply the general public with information presented in a colorful, entertaining and understandable way, while focusing on the ultimate goals of promoting public awareness of the existence, importance of China's rich and diverse wild mammalian resources; promoting public awareness of the plight of many of these species and

1

the critical need to protect and sustain these resources; and promoting public support for and cooperation in protecting those resources. Secondly, it aims to become a basic reference source for administrators in forestry, public security, railways, airports, harbors and industry and commence organizations as a guide for wildlife law enforcement and species identification. Thirdly, it hopes to serve as a useful guide for tourists and foreign visitors interested in wildlife and wildlife conservation in China. Finally, it is hoped that Mammalian of China will help to popularize interest in and love for wildlife and wildlife conservation throughout China.

Mammalian of China contains 534 species of mammals occurring in China. Of these, 193 species, mostly those of the major large and medium – sized protected species, are introduced as representative of their families. Color distribution maps and full – color photos of each representative species are included, along with scientific name, English name, classification, characteristics, habitats, reproduction , distribution and conservation status. Fifteen other species are described with color distribution maps. The remaining species are described only by their scientific name. Throughout the book, mammalian nomenclature and classification follow the taxonomy used in the following references: *A World List of Mammalian Species*. (Corbet, G. B. and Hill, J. E., 3rd Ed., 1991); *The Mammals of Indomalayan Region: A systematic Review*. (Corbet and Hill, 1992); *The Distribution of Mammalian Species in China*. (Zhang Yongzhu, 1997) and the unpublished manuscript entitled *Outline of Mammalian Species in China* by Wang Yinxiang and Zhung Chanlin. The book is arranged first by Order then by Family and finally by Species. The individual species marked with an asterisk (*) are those representative species described in length throughout the book. Provided for each species is an abbreviated symbol denoting the conservation status assigned to that species, the assigning authority, (i. e. Wildlife Protection *Law of the People' sRepublic of China*; IUCN's red list of threatened and endangered animals; CITES appendices), and the conservation parameters assigned to each status. Symbols and categories include the following:

China I   Category One species, as defined by the Wildlife Protection Law of the People's Republic of China. Hunting of species banned without permission from the Ministry of Forestry

China II   Category Two species, as defined by the Wildlife Protection Law of the people's Republic of China. Hunting of species allowed with permission of the Forestry Department at provincial level

    CR   Critically endangered species, as defined by the International Union for Conservation of Nature and Natural Resources (IUCN). Species in critical danger of extinction; survival unlikely if cause factors persist

    EN   Endangered species, as defined by the IUCN. Species in danger of extinction; survival unlikely if cause factors persist

    VU   Vulnerable species, as defined by the IUCN. Species likely to become endangered in the near feature

    Appendix I   As defined by Appendix I of the Convention on International Trade in Endangered Species of Wild Fauna and Flora (CITES). Forbids all commercial trade in species

    Appendix II   As defined by Appendix II of the Convention on International Trade in Endangered Species of Wild Fauna and Flora (CITES). Refers to species that would become extinct if trade is not regulated; CITES sets quota and permit requirements for commercial trade in these species.

    The authors wish to express their deepest appreciation to Professor Xu Hongfa, and Drs. Wang Xiaoming, Zhang Endi, and Li Ming for their invaluable assistance in the preparation of and support for this book. We also graciously thank Vice Editor-in-Chief, Mr. Chen Li, and Editor, Ms. Li Wei, of the China Forestry Publishing House who kindly advised and guided us through the publishing procedure. Additional thanks goes out to Professors Wang Yingxiang and Zheng Changlin who supported us to use some of their unpublished material. Finally, we wish express our thanks to our many colleagues and friends who have provided us photographs, information and moral support throughout this endeavor.

The Authors

Sheng Helin

Noriyuki Ohtaishi

Lu Houji

CONTENTS

1

CONTENTS

CONTENTS

3

CONTENTS

4

CONTENTS

ORDERS AND NUMBER OF SPECIES OF MAMMALS IN CHINA

There are 21 orders and 4327 species living in the world (Corbet &Hill 1991). China has 14 orders and 534 species. The orders and number of species are listed as follows:

INSECTIVORA	61 species
SCANDENTIA	1 species
CHIROPTERA	98 species
PRIMATES	21 species
CARNIVORA	54 species
PINNIPEDIA	5 species
CETACEA	31 species
SIRENIA	1 species
PROBOSCIDEA	1 species
PERISSODACTYLA	2 species
ARTIODACTYLA	44 species
PHOLIDOTA	1 species
RODENTIA	185 species
LAGOMORPHA	29 species

There are several species of mammals such as the nutria, (*Myocastor coypus*), reindeer (*Rangifer tarandus*) and the mithan (*Bos frontalis*), which are not native to China. They were introduced and now are semi-domesticated and occasionally found in the wild.

INSECTIVORA

The insectivores are the most primitive living species of the Chinese mammals, most of the species are relatively small, and mouselike in appearance with long pointed flexible snouts. The ears and eyes are small. The limbs are short. The postorbital processes are undeveloped, the orbits open posteriorly and are not bordered posteriorly by a postorbital bar. They have more than 26 sharp teeth. The males have abdominal testes. Insectivores can live above ground or underground. They primarily feed on insects and helminths. There are 6 families and 356 species living in the world of which China has 3 families and 61 species.

Erinaceidae	7	species
Soricidae	41	species
Talpidae	13	species

Erinaceidae

Erinaceidae members are relatively large in size for insectivora. The pelage is soft or specialized into spines. There are 9 genera and 19 species in the world, of these China has 3 genera and 7 species. The species are as follows:

Hylomys suillus
* Hylomys sinensis
Hylomys hainanensis
* Erinaceus amurensis

* Hemiechinus auritus
* Hemiechinus dauuricus
Hemiechinus hughi

Newborn Amur hedgehog

Defense behavior of a hedgehog

Hylomys sinensis Shrew hedgehog

Description Head and body 10 – 13 cm, tail 6 – 8 cm, and weight 44 – 60g. The pelage on the back is dark brown and the back has no black dorsal stripe.

Habits Inhabits tropical evergreen forests. Burrows under roots of trees or fernery. Their activities are confined to the forest edge. Feeds on various insects and a variety of roots and stems.

Reproduction The young are born in April to May after a gestation period of 30 – 35 days. There are 4 – 5 young in a litter.

Distribution Sichuan, Yunnan and Guizhou.

Erinaceus amurensis Amur hedgehog

Description Head and body 22 – 26cm, tail 2 – 4 cm, and weight 600 – 1000 g. Except the underparts and limbs, entire body is covered with sharp and hard spines. The ears are short about 2 cm long.

Habits Inhabits forests, grasslands, cultivated lands and a variety of habitats. Shelters among rock crevices, under dense bunchshrubs, and in ruinous heaps or burrows along canals. Feeds mainly on insects and small vertebrates. It also infests fruits, legumes, and melon crops. It is nocturnal and hibernates from October to late March.

Reproduction Mating occurs after emergence from hibernation. Gestation is about 7 weeks and births take place in June. One litter per year, and the litter size is usually 3 – 6, occasionally as large as 8. At birth, the young are covered with short and thick soft spines. The animals are fully grown and sexually mature in the second year of life. In captivity the animal may live up to 7 years.

Distribution Eastern China and northeast China.

Hylomys sinensis

Erinaceus amurensis

5

Hemiechinus auritus

Long-eared hedgehog

Description Head and body 17 – 22 cm, tail 2.5 – 3.5 cm, and weight 280 – 500 g. Body covered with hard spines except on underparts and limbs. The back spines are long as 3 cm. The ears are long and reach about 4 cm.

Habits Inhabits semi-desert areas, but sometimes are found around farm lands.

This animal is solitary and nocturnal, usually uses other animals burrow for nesting. Feeds on small rodents, lizards, insects and carrion, but also eats vegetables and melons. Hibernates in winter.

Reproduction Mating usually occurs in spring and in summer. Gestation lasts 35 – 42 days and a litter of 2 – 6 young are born. The young are sexually mature in the second year.

Distribution Xinjiang, Nei Mongol, Gansu, Ningxia.

Hemiechinus dauuricus Daurian hedgehog

Description Head and body approximately 25 cm, tail 2 – 3 cm, and weight about 500 g. Ears are about 3 cm, and are longer than the spines surrounding them. The body is covered with hard spines except the underparts and limbs. The dorsal spines are about 2 cm in length.

Habits Inhabits steppes, sand dunes and willows plots. The animal uses rodents bur-

rows for their nest. Feeds on rodents, lizards, insects and a variety of small sized animals, it also feeds on vegetable matter. Hibernates in winter.

Reproduction Mating occurs in spring. Annually a single litter of 3 – 7 young are born in June and July. The young reach sexual maturity in 1 year.

Distribution Northeast and north China.

Hemiechinus auritus

Hemiechinus dauuricus

INSECTIVORA

Soricidae

The shrews are small, mouselike insectivores with long pointed snouts. The feet are not well developed and the claws are small. The eyes and ears are relatively small. The first pair of incisors are well developed. The shrews are agile in their movements. Most of the species prefer moist situations. Feeds mainly on insects and a variety of small invertebrates, they also take seeds and legumes. There are 21 families and 272 species in the world. China has 10 families and 41 species. The recognized species are:

Sorex asper
Sorex bedfordiae
* Sorex caecutiens
Sorex cansulus
Sorex cylindricauda
Sorex daphaenodon
Sorex excelsus
Sorex gracillimus
Sores isodon
Sorex mirabilis
Sorex minutissimus
* Sorex minutus
Sorex sinalis
Sorex thibetanus
Sorex unguiculatus
Soriculus caudatus
Soriculus fumidus
Soriculus hypsibius
Soriculus lamula
Soriculus leucops
Soriculus macrurus

Soriculus nigrescens
Soriculus sacratus
Soriculus salenskii
Soriculus parca
Soriculus smithii
Neomys fodiens
Blarinella quadraticauda
Crocidura attenuata
Crocidura fuliginosa
Crocidura guldenskedtii
Crocidura horsfieldi
Crocidura lasiura
Crocidura russula
Crocidura sibirica
* Crocidura suaveolens
Suncus etruscus
* Suncus murinus
Anourosorex squamipes
Chimarogale himalayica
Chimarogale styani
Nectogale elegans

Sorex minutus Eurasian pygmy shrew

Description Head and body 4 – 6 cm, tail 3 – 5 cm, and weight only 3 – 7 g. This species is one of the smallest mammals. The upper parts are brown and underparts brownish gray. The dorsal tail is same as the body color and the ventral part a distinct grayish white. In the specimens of Xizang, the tail color is less distinctive.

Habits Inhabits forests, shrubs and bunch grass areas near forest edges. This small creature shelters in burrows. They are active by day and night. Feeds on insects, larvae, earthworms and small invertebrates. This species does not hibernate in winter.

Reproduction Mating occurs from spring to summer, the gestation period is 24 – 25 days. There are 1 – 2 litters a year, litter size 4 – 8. The life span is 14 – 15 months.

Distribution Eastern Nei Mongol, western Xingjiang, western Xizang, Gansu and Sichuan.

Sorex caecutiens Laxmann's shrew

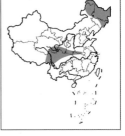

Description Head and body 5 – 7 cm, tail 3 – 4 cm, and weight 7.6 – 9 g. The pelage is brown dorsally, underparts pale brownish yellow or yellowish white. The tail is distinctly bicolored, the upper part is same as the back and the underpart is same as the abdominal.

Habits Inhabits forests, shrubs and grasslands. In Xizang, they are found in grass lands bordering montane deciduous forests up to an altitude of 3800 m. Feeds on insects and land invertebrates.

Reproduction Mating occurs from May to September. Gestation lasts 35 days. There are 2 litters in a year and the litter size 2 – 8.

Distribution Northeast China, Sichuan and Xizang.

Sorex minutus

Sorex caecutiens

Crocidura suaveolens
Lesser white-toothed shrew

Description Head and body 5.1 – 6.6 cm, tail 3.0 – 3.8 cm, and weight 5.7 – 7.1 g. The limbs are slender, the tail fringed with short and long sparsely hair. The incisors are white; the eyes are small and having a long pointed snout with long whiskers.

Habits Inhabits grasslands, forests, wilderness and other types of habitats. The animals live in burrows and are active in the night. Feeds on insects, earthworms, snails and invertebrates. Because of its small size they are active throughout the night foraging for food. The daily amount of intake is heavier than its body weight. Mating occurs in late spring to early autumn. Gestation lasts 24 – 32 days. There are 2 litters a year, each with 3 – 7 young.

Distribution Northeast China, east China, north China, and northwest of Xinjiang.

Suncus murinus House shrew

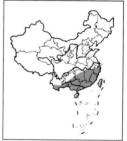

Description Head and body 9 – 14 cm, tail 4.7 – 8.3 cm, and weight 30 – 85 g. A mouselike creature with a long snout. Pelage gray, the tail thick at the base, the tail is fringed with short and long sparse hairs. The animals have well developed scent glands on the flanks.

Habits Inhabits cultivated lands of plain areas, along shores, marsh lands, shrubs, grass areas, vegetable gardens and inside farm houses. The shrews are active at night. Feeds on insects, larvae, earthworms, but it also eats plant seeds and small rodents.

Reproduction Mating extends from March to October. The gestation period is 20 days. Two to three litters per year with a litter size of 1 – 7, usually 3 – 7 per litter. Sexual maturity at 6 weeks. Life span is 1.5 – 2.5 years.

Distribution Southern China.

Crocidura suaveolens

Suncus murinus

INSECTIVORA

Talpidae

Moles are of small size and tubular-shaped. The muzzle is long, the eyes are small, and there are no external ears. The neck is short and thick. In the genus talpa, the forefeet have specialized into large palms and are rotated so that the palms face outward. The forefeet are armed with large and broad claws adapted for digging. The animals live underground, rarely come to the surface and are active at day and night. Feeds on insects, helminths and other small invertebrates. The fur is thick, solf, dense and velvety. There are 12 families and 42 species of which China has 4 families and 13 species.

Uropsilus andersoni
Uropsilus gracilis
Uropsilus soricipes
Euroscaptor grandis
Euroscaptor longirostris
Euroscaptor micrura
* Parascaptor leucura

Scaptochirus moschatus
Mogera insularis
Mogera robusta
Mogera wogura
Scaptonyx fusicaudus
Scapanulus oweni

Parascaptor leucura White-tailed mole

Description Head and body 8.2 – 11 cm, tail 1.5 – 3 cm, and weight 30 – 50 g. The snout is pointed and grooved on the top. The forefeet are stocky; the palms broad and flat with strong spade shaped claws. The sticklike tail is short, sparsely covered with short white hair. The fur is soft and fine, with a sheeny grayish black color.

Habits Inhabits forests at altitudes below 1000 m. It lives underground in soft soils. It forages by digging with its forefeet palms. Feeds on various insects and other invertebrates.

Reproduction Mating occurs in spring. Gestation lasts about 28 days. Females produce 1 – 2 litters per year. Usually 2 – 7 per litter.

Distribution Western Yunnan and southern Sichuan.

Parascaptor leucura

SCANDENTIA

All the species of the order are squirrel-like. Although externally they look like squirrels, biologically their features are not related with rodentia. They were formerly classed as insectivora or considered primates. In the eighties of this century zoologists agreed that they are independent and are now placed in an order of their own, Scandentia. Tree shrews are all of one family (Tupaiidae) with 16 species. Only one species is native to China.

Tupaia belangeri Northern tree shrew

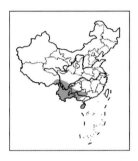

Description Head and body 16 – 18 cm, tail 15 – 19 cm, and weight 110 – 185 g. The snout is pointed and long, the eyes are large, the ears are short and rounded. The tail is covered with short hair on the dorsal and ventral parts, and long hair on the sides, giving the impression that the tail is flat. The tail is olive brown above, the underside dirty white. The sides of the neck have two yellow stripes

Habits Inhabits mountains, hillylands, plain areas, shrubs, forest edges, rock crevices and near villages located in tropical and subtropical forests. They are good climbers, runnning about on trees and shrubs, and forage on the ground. They are active by day and night, but most active in the morning and evening. Feeds on insects, small birds and bird's eggs, mice, and also fruits and seeds.

Reproduction Mating occurs in March to August. The estrous period is 8 – 10 days, gestation lasts 41 – 46 days. The females produce 2 litters per year, each litter contains 2 – 4 young.

Distribution Yunnan, Guangxi and Hainan.

Tupaia belangeri

CHIROPTERA

Chiroptera species are the world's only true flying group of mammals. The forefeet are specialized into wings, the palm and finger bones are very long. The lengths of the third fingers are as long as the head and body. A hairy thin wing membrane extends from the shoulders, forelimbs, nails end, sides of the body and tail. The 5 toes of the hind legs have sharp curved claws, which are used for hanging when they are resting or sleeping. Bats are active mostly in the evening and at night. Most bats hibernate in the winter. There are 18 families and 1000 species in the world of these China has 7 families and about 99 species. The 7 families are:

Pteropodiae	9	species
Emballonuride	1	species
Megadermatidae	1	species
Rhinolophidae	13	species
Hipposideridae	9	species
Vespertilionidae	63	species
Molossidae	2	species

Pteropodidae

A large size bat with a fox like face. The eyes are large. The external ears simple with no tragus. The crowns of the teeth are smooth. Feeds on fruits and other vegetable matter. There are 162 species in the world of which 9 species are found in China.

Rousettus amplexicaudatus	*Cynopterus brachyotis*
* *Rousettus leschenaulti*	*Cynopterus sphinx*
* *Pteropus dasymallus*	*Sphaerias blanfordi*
Pteropus giganteus	*Eonycteris spelaea*
Pteropus lylei	

Pteropus dasymallus Ryukyu flying fox

Description Head and body about 20 cm, ear 2 cm and wing span 70cm. There is no tail. The body is covered with blackish brown fur, the forehead gray, the back of the neck yellow or grayish yellow. The dorsal fur long and soft about 3 cm in length. The shoulders have golden yellow or milkish white circles.

Habits Inhabits tropical forest regions. Active in night, by day it hangs on trees in colonies. Feeds on various fruits.

Reproduction Mating occurs in July to October. Females produce one litter per year and bear a single young in March. Gestation is about 140 – 150 days. The life span is long in this genus, some species have lived in captivity up to 31 years.

Distribution Taiwan. Very rare.

Conservation CITES: appendix II.

Rousettus leschenaulti
Leschenault's rousette

Description Head and body 9 – 13 cm, tail 1 – 2 cm, and weight 80 – 120 g. Tail tip is separate from the interfemoral membrane. Body color is dark brown.

Habits A typically tropical forest species, cave dwelling, boosts in clusters. In Hainan Province it boosts in large colonies up to thousands. Feeds on various berries and pollen.

Reproduction Bears a single young in May to June. In Hainan this species may give birth at time in spring and in autumn. In Guangxi a single young is born from May to June. Gestation is about 125 days. The males are sexual maturity at 5 months of age and the females at 15 months of age.

Distribution Southern parts of China.

Rousettus leschenaulti

Pteropus dasymallus

19

CHIROPTERA

Emballonuridae

This order is characterized by that the tail base is completely enclosed in the tail membrane and the tail tip penetrates the tail membrane upwards from the back. There are 13 genera and 49 species in the world. China has 1 species.

* *Taphozous melanopogon*

Taphozous melanopogon
Black-bearded tomb bat

Description Head and body 7.5 – 8.5 cm, tail 3 cm, and weight 30 – 40 g. The adult male has black tufts on the chin. There is no toe on the second finger. The tail tip penetrates from the back of the interfemoral membrane. The color of the body is usually tan brown.

Habits Inhabits tropical areas. They are cave dwellers and roost in caves in groups. Often associated with Himalayan leaf nosed bats, but the two species have their own roosting sites. Feeds on various insects.

Reproduction Produce a single young in summer.

Distribution From south of southern Quizhou to Hainan.

Taphozous melanopogon

CHIROPTERA

Megadermatidae

This family consists of large sized bats with a wing span about 100 cm. The ears are large, united by skin folds, and with a divided tragus. The nose leaf is narrow with a long projection upward from the tip of the snout. The tail is short or absent. There are four genera and 5 species in the world. China has only one species.

Megaderma lyra Greater false vampire

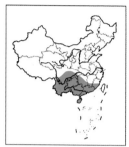

Description Head and body 89 – 95 cm, the forearm length is about 7 cm, and weight 50 – 70 g. There is no tail. The nose leaf is well developed; the ears are large with rounded tips, length about 4 cm, the tragus is fork shaped. The pelage is dense, grayish brown dorsally and the underparts are paler.

Habits Inhabit caves of broadleaf forest at altitudes of 850 – 1500 m. These bats are nocturnal and roost by day in small groups of 20 – 30 individuals. Feeds on rodents, small birds, frogs, insects and other bats as well.

Reproduction Mating occurs in late autumn to early winter. Gestation lasts about 5 – 6 months, usually gives birth to 1 young, but occasionally 2. The young are weaned at about 3 months. The females reach sexually mature at 19 months of age and the males at 15 months.

Distribution Southern parts of China.

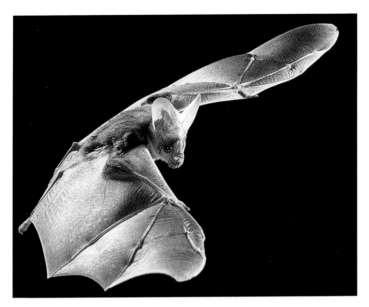

Megaderma lyra

A Greater false vampire with captured prey

CHIROPTERA

Rhinolophidae

Members of this family have a complex nose leaf and lack a tragus. The toes of the hingleg consist of 3 bones. These bats roost in colonies in caves or in tree cavities. Feeds on insects. There is only one genus and 64 species in the world. There are 13 species in China.

Rhinolophus affinis
Rhinolophus cornutus
Rhinolophus ferrumequinum
Rhinolophus lepidus
Rhinolophus luctus
Rhinolophus macrotis
Rhinolophus monoceros

Rhinolophus pearsoni
Rhinolophus pusillus
Rhinolophus rex
* Rhinolophus rouxii
Rhinolophus thomsai
Rhinolophus yunanensis

Rhinolophus rouxii
Rouxi's horseshoe bat

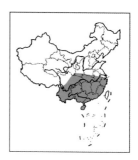

Description Head and body 5.1 – 5.7 cm, tail 2.4 – 2.6 cm, forearm 4.4 – 5.0 cm and weight 11 – 14 g. The dorsal body color is brown.

Habits Roosts together in large colonies in moist caves. It often associates and shares its quarters with Schreiber's long fingered bats and Little Japanese horse bats. The bats forage at night for nocturnal insects. It hibernates in mid November in eastern China and when it emerges in spring, it has loss 26.8 % of its body weight.

Reproduction Mating occurs in autumn. A single young is born in June. They become mature at 2 years of age.

Distribution South of Qinling Mts range.

Rhinolophus rouxii

Bat at roost

CHIROPTERA

Hipposideridae

All these species are similar to Horseshoe bats, which have a complicated nose leaf and lack a tragus, but in these bats the toes of the hindfeet have only 2 bones. There are 9 genera and 64 species found in the world of these China has 9 species.

* *Hipposideros armiger*
  Hipposideros bicolor
  Hipposideros fulvus
  Hipposideros larvatus
  Hipposideros lylei

  Hipposideros pomona
  Hipposideros pratti
  Aselliscus stoliczkanus
  Coelops frithi

Hipposideros armiger
Himalayan leaf-nosed bat

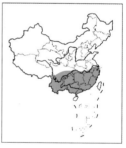

Description Head and body 8 – 11 cm, tail 4.5 – 6.5 cm, forearm 8 – 9 cm, and weight 50 – 70 g. The Himalayan leaf nosed bat is one of the largest bats in the family. The pelage is fine and dense, color brown above and the underparts are paler.

Habits Roost in caves and temples, associate in large groups and share quarters with bats of other species. In evening the bats catch their insect prey in flight. Hibernates in winter in large colonies.

Reproduction In China, this species bears a single young, sometimes twins in May to June. Sexual maturity is reached in the second year.

Distribution South of Yangzi River.

Hipposideros armiger(♂)

Hipposideros armiger(♀)

27

CHIROPTERA

Vespertilionidae

This family form the largest numbers of the order Chiroptera. Relatively small in body size and weigh from 5 – 45 g. This family have a tragus but lack of nose leaf. They have complete interfermoral membranes. The length of the tail is longer than the head and body. The tail is covered by the interfemoral membrane or only the tail tip extends outward of the membrane. There are about 350 species to this family and at least 63 species occur in China.

Myotis adversus
Myotis altarium
Myotis annectans
Myotis blythii
Myotis brandti
Myotis chinensis
Myotis dasycneme
Myotis daubentoni
Myotis fimbriatus
Myotis formosus
Myotis frater
Myotis horsfieldii
Myotis ikonnikovi
Myotis montivagus
Myotis muricola
Myotis myotis
Myotis mystacinus
Myotis nattereri
Myotis pequinius
* Myotis ricketti
Myotis siligorensis
Pipistrellus abramus
Pipistrellus affinis
Pipistrellus ceylonicus
Pipistrellus circumfatus
Pipistrellus coromandra
Pipistrellus javanicus
Pipistrellus kuhlii
Pipistrellus mimus
Pipistrellus paterculus
* Pipistrellus pipistrellus
Pipistrellus pulveratus

Pipistrellus savii
Scotozous dormeri
Eptesicus nilssonii
Eptesicus serotinus
Ia io
Nyctalus aviator
* Nyctalus noctula
Vespertilio murinus
Vespertilio orientalis
Vespertilio superans
Tylonycteris pachypus
Tylonycteris robustula
Scotomanes ornatus
Scotophilus heathii
Scotophilus kuhlii
Barbastella leucomelas
Plecotus austriacus
* Plecotus auritus
Miniopterus australio
Miniopterus magnater
Miniopterus pusillus
Miniopterus schreibersii
Murina aurata
Murina cyclotis
Murina huttoni
Murina leucogaster
Murina puta
Murina rubex
Kerivoula hardwickei
Kerivoual picta
Harpiocephalus harpia

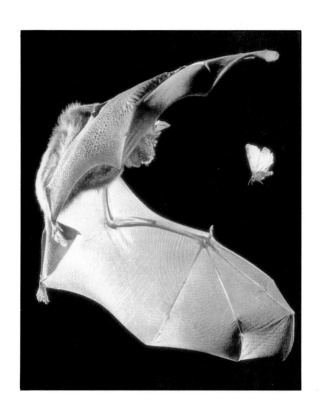

Myotis ricketti
Rickett's big-footed bat

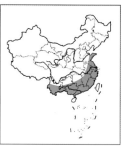

Description Head and body 6.7 – 7.0 cm, tail 5.0 – 5.3 cm, forearm 5.6 – 5.8 cm, and weight 20 – 23 g. The feet are large, about 2 cm in length. The coat is smoky brown above and grayish white beneath.

Habits Inhabits hilly lands and montane areas. Roosts in colonies in caves and in crevices of old city walls. It associates with bats of other species. The bats are active and forage for insects at night. These bats do not migrate, but goes into hibernation for winter.

Reproduction Mating occurs during late autumn and early winter. Gives birth to a single young in the second year of June.

Distribution Southeast China.

Pipistrellus pipistrellus
Common pipistrelle

Description Head and body 3.6 – 4.1 cm, forearm 3.1 – 3.3 cm, and weight 4 – 4.5 g. The ears and tragus are short. The tail is shorter than the length of the head and body, and the tail tip is covered by the interfemoral membrane. The fur color is black above and blackish brown beneath.

Habits Roosts singly under eaves and also in caves. Pipistrelles are active throughout the night, and it is found near human settlements and in open areas of ponds, paddy fields and lakes. Feeds on flying insects, mainly eats mosquitoes caught in flight. This species hibernates in winter and emerges in April.

Reproduction Usually two young are born in June, in Zhejiang. Gestation period is 25 – 30 days, lactation lasts 20 – 30 days. The young are sexual maturity at 12 months of age.

Distribution Distribute throughout southern China.

Myotis ricketti

Pipistrellus pipistrellus

31

CHIROPTERA

Nyctalus noctula Noctule bat

Description Head and body 6.8 – 7.6 cm, tail 4.6 – 5.0 cm, forearm 4.7 – 5.3 cm, and weight 18 – 30 g. The ears are short and broad. The fur is dense and brown in color.

Habits Roost in old buildings such as under eaves, ceilings, crevices of walls and in hollows of trees. Noctule bats form roost colonies numbering from dozens to more than hundreds. It forages at dusk and throughout the night. Feeds mainly on nocturnal winged insects while flying.

Reproduction Mating occurs before hibenation, the sperms are stored in the uterus of the female where it remains viable during the winter. Ovulation and fertilization occur after emerge from hibernation, with a gestation period of 50 – 60 days. The young are born in May and June, with a litter size of 2. The lactation period is about 20 days. The young bats are sexually mature before hibernation.

Distribution South of Shandong and Shaanxi.

Plecotus auritus Brown long-eared bat

Description Head and body 5 cm, tail 5 cm, and weight about 7 g. The ears are very large with a length of 3.7 cm. The tragus is long and narrow. The body is grayish brown above and the underparts rather pale.

Habits Roost in hollows of trees, roofs of buildings, crevices of remaining walls. These bats do not live in large colonies. Feeds on flying insects. Hibernates from September to October and e-merges during April to May.

Reproduction Mating occurs in autumn. The gestation period is 56 – 100 days. The speed of embryonic development is dependent on the body temperature. Females give birth from spring to summer. Once a year a single litter of 1 – 2 is produced.

Distribution North China, northeast China and northwest China.

Nyctalus noctula

Plecotus auritus

Molossidae

This family is characterized externally by a doglike facial feature, the muzzle is large and broad. There are 12 genera and 89 species in the world, of these 2 species occur in China.

Tadarida plicata   * *Tadarida teniotis*

Head showing the doglike facial feature

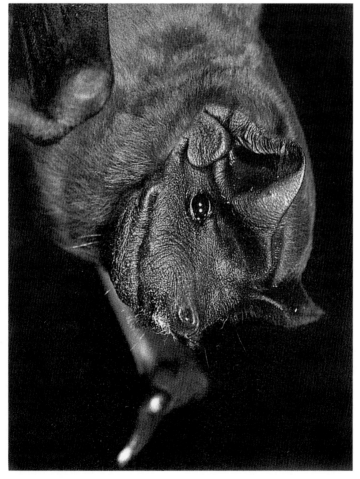

Tadarida teniotis
European free-tailed bat

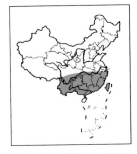

Description Head and body 9 cm, tail 5.5 cm, ear 3.1 cm, and weight 32 – 34 g. The ears are large and broad, the length and width of the ears are almost equal. The tail extends from the back edge of interfemoral membrane. The pelage is brown or grayish brown.

Habits. Roosts alone or in small groups of 2 – 3 Individuals together in caves, it does not associate with bats of other species. Feeds on nocturnal insects. It hibernates. In southern Anhui Proivnce, the species hibernates from October to March.

Reproduction Mating occurs in autumn, usually one young is born in summer and sexual maturity is attained in the second year.

Distribution Southern China.

Tadarida teniotis

35

PRIMATES

Although the evolution of living primates groups are at different levels, the mutual characteristics of primates are: The four limbs are adapted for living in trees, thus aids in climbing or walking on the ground; The fingers and toes are relatively long, in the lower forms some certain sharp fingers and toes have developed into flat nails. In the higher forms all the fingers and toes have developed into flat nails, the soles and the digits are sensitive; The great toes and the thumbs are opposable, which makes the hands and feet efficient for grasping and climbing; The eyes are directed forward. Primates inhabit tropical and subtropical forest areas. There are 10 families and about 180 species in the world in the suborders of Prosimii and Anthropoidae. China has 3 families and 21 species. They are:

Lorisidae	3	species
Cercopithecidae	14	species
Hylobatidae	4	species

Lorisidae

Prosimians are relatively primitive forms of primates. The main characteristic is that certain digits remain claws and the other digits have developed into nails. They have short foxy muzzle and large face, forward owlish eyes, the tail is short or absent. The species of this family are arboreal and nocturnal and slow in locomotion There are 16 species in the world of which China has 3 species.

* *Nycticebus coucang*
* *Nycticebus intermedius*

* *Nycticebus pygmaeus*

Nycticebus coucang Slow loris

Description Head and body 26 – 38 cm, tail 1 – 2 cm, and weight 1.2 – 2.0 kg. The first digit of each limb is opposable to the other digits. The second digit toe of the feet has a sharp claw and the other digits have flattened nails. The pelage is soft, thick and dense. The dorsal part is dark brown or yellowsh brown with a dark brown dorsal stripe along the back. The tip of the nose and around the sides of the eyes are brown.

Habits Inhabits primeval tropical and subtropical forests. It is arboreal, solitary and nocturnal, sheltering by day in hollow trees, slow in motion and seldom comes to the ground. Feeds mainly on fruits and insects, but also eats small birds and bird's eggs.

Reproduction Breeds throughout the year. Estrous cycle 37 – 54 days, gestation lasts 93 days and weaned at 3.5 months. Litter size usually 1, occasionally 2. Life span in captivity is 13 – 14 years.

Distribution Yunnan and southern Guangxi. Rare with a population about 1500 – 2000 individuals in the wild.

Conservation China: I; CITES: appendix II.

Nycticebus coucang

Nycticebus pygmaeus
Lesser slow loris

Description Head and body 21 – 23 cm, tail about 1 cm, and weight 250 – 450 g. The face is rounded and the ears are large. The fur is soft, dense and woolly, reddish brown in color with whitish gray tips, there is no dark dorsal stripe along the back. There are white stripes running from the nose to the forehead.

Habits Inhabits northern fringes of tropical rain forests. This species is an arboreal dwellers, which seldom descends to the ground. In the day it sleeps in small groups curled up tightly like a ball in the trees. They are omnivorous, at dust the animal moves slowly among the tree branches hunting for food.

Reproduction Little is known about its reproduction, probably similar to the slow loris. The young are born in February and March. The lactation period is 30 – 36 days.

Distribution Southern parts of Yunnan, only a few hundred in the wild.

Conservation China: I; IUCN: V; CITES: appendix II.

Nycticebus intermedius
Intermediate slow loris

Description Head and body 24 – 26 cm, tail very short, and weight 500 – 800 g. The fur is woolly and silky, dull brown in color and the guard hair tipped with white giving appearance of frostlike cover. There is a dark color dorsal stripe running along the back.

Habits Inhabits northern fringes of south east Asia rain forests or monsoon forests. They are arboreal and nocturnal. Feeds chiefly on insects, small animals and fruits.

Reproduction The young are born in the months of February to March. Two young per litter, the lactation period is 15 – 20 weeks.

Distribution Southern Yunnan. About 200000 individuals are currently surviving in the wild.

Conservation China: I; CITES: appendix II.

Nycticebus pygmaeus

Nycticebus intermedius

PRIMATES

Cercopithecidae

The more advanced primates are in the suborder Anthropoidea. The major characteristics are: The fingers and toes of many primates have developed into flat nails. The eyes facing forward, and there is considerable development of the brain. Most primates have long tails, are arboreal or terrestrial, capable of rapid locomotion and diurnal in habits. There are about 80 species in the world. China has 3 genera and 14 species. As for *Pygathrix memaeus* there is no record to prove that it has ever existed in China. The species of Cercopithecidae are as follows.

* *Macaca arctoides*
* *Macaca assamensis*
* *Macaca cyclopis*
* *Macaca mulatta*
* *Macaca nemestrina*
* *Macaca thibetana*
* *Pygathrix brelichi*

* *Pygathrix roxellana*
* *Pygathrix bieti*
  Semnopithecus francoisi
  Semnopithecus geei
  Semnopithecus pileatus
* *Semnopithecus phayrei*
* *Semnopithecus entellus*

Macaca nemestrina Pig-tailed macaque

Description Head and body about 60 cm, tail 15 – 18 cm, and weight 11 – 14 kg. It has short, smooth black hair on the top of the head and short whiskers on the sides of the face. The pelage is brown or dull brown above and grayish white below. Sometimes there is a blackish brown midline stripe along the back, which extends to the base of the tail. The tail is short and slender that slightly curls like a pig.

Habits Inhabits dense evergreen forest. These animals move in groups lead by a large adult as leader. Feeds on fruits and seeds.

Reproduction The mean estrous cycle of the female is 43 days, the gestation period is 171（162 – 186）days. Females produce 1 young and lactation is about 3 months. Sexual maturity takes 4 years. Under captivity the life span may reach 26 years.

Distribution Southern Yunnan, with a population of 1000 individuals.

Conservation China: I; IUCN: VU; CITES: appendix II.

Head of the Pig – tailed macaque

Macaca nemestrina

Macaca mulatta Rhesus macaque

Description Head and body 51 – 60, tail 20 – 30 cm, and weight 3 – 6 kg. The face and the ears are flesh colored. The callositas ischialis (horny area) on the rump is red. The pelage is brownish gray or brownish yellow above and light gray below. Cheek pouches are present which acts temporal storage of food.

Habits Inhabits mountain forest of subtropical and tropical areas. The rhesus monkey are arboreal and diurnal in habit, sometimes it comes to the ground. Group size usually varies from 20 – 30 individuals, but a large group numbering 60 – 100 individuals may occur. The dominant male leads and defends the group. Feeds on various kinds of fruits, flowers and tender buds, when lack of food it also takes barks, roots and stems of plants.

Reproduction Mating occurs from November to December. The species are seasonally breeders, births occur from March to June. The estrus cycle is about 28 days, with a heat period of 1 – 4 days. The gestation period is about 163 days, the lactation period is 4 months. The females attain sexual maturity at 2.5 – 3 years, but the young females do not have their first offspring until they reach 4 years of age. The males reach sexual maturity at the age of 4 – 5 year. The life span in captivity may reach 30 years.

Distribution Shanxi, southern Shaanxi, and central and southern China. The population is about 300 000.

Conservation China: II; CITES: appendix II.

Rhesus macaque of Hainan Province

Macaca mulatta

PRIMATES

Macaca cyclopis Taiwan macaque

Description Head and body 36 – 45 cm, and weight 4 – 5 kg. The males are slightly larger than the females. The body color is grayish brown above, and below grayish white. The limbs dull gray and the forehead is naked.

Habits Inhabits forests and grasslands in coastal areas, due to human activities the species is now restricted to montane forest areas. The monkeys reside in caves or among rocks. It lives in family groups of 5 – 6, but can number up to 30 – 50 individuals. Most active in the morning and in the evening, and rest in caves at midday. Feeds on berries, tender leaves, insects, crustaceans and mollusks.

Reproduction Breeds throughout the year. The gestation period is about 6 months and produces a single offspring. The longevity of captive individuals is about 20 years.

Distribution Taiwan. The population is estimated to be about 7000 individuals in the wild.

Conservation China: I; IUCN: VU; CITES: appendix II.

Macaca cyclopis

Macaca arctoides Bear macaque

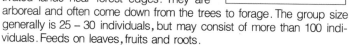

Description Head and body 51 – 65 cm, tail short only 5 cm, and weight 10 – 15.5 kg. The females are smaller than the males. The color of the body is grayish brown to dull brown. The forehead and cheeks have short and sparse hair, the face is dull red in color.

Habits Inhabits forests and also around cultivated lands near forest edges. They are arboreal and often come down from the trees to forage. The group size generally is 25 – 30 individuals, but may consist of more than 100 individuals. Feeds on leaves, fruits and roots.

Reproduction Breeding occurs throughout the year. Average estrous cycle length is 30.7 days, gestation 177.5 days. The age of sexual maturity is 3 – 4 years in females and 5 years in males. The longevity is about 25 years.

Distribution Guangdong, Guangxi, Guizhou and Yunnan. There are about 50 000 – 80 000 individuals.

Conservation China: II; IUCN: VU; CITES: appendix II.

Macaca assamensis Assam macaque

Description Head and body 56 – 65 cm, tail 23 – 25 cm, and weight 12 – 14 kg. The body shape resembles the rhesus monkeys, but stoutly built. The body color is brown. The face is flesh colored.

Habits Inhabits throughout tropical and subtropical forests. Lives in groups of 10 – 30 individuals. Arboreal, they spend most of their time moving in large trees and seldom descend to the ground. Feeds mainly on plant matter, includes fruit, roots, stems, tree barks and also ingest insects.

Reproduction Little is known about its reproduction, most of the young are born in spring.

Distribution Yunnan, Guangxi and Xizang. With a population of 10000 individuals in the wild.

Conservation China: II; IUCN: VU; CITES: appendix II.

Macaca arctoides

Macaca assamensis

Macaca thibetana
Chinese stump-tailed macaque

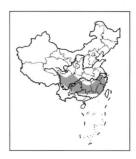

Description Head and body 58 – 71 cm, tail 7 – 14 cm and weight 14 – 17.5 kg, but may weigh in excess of 32kg. The females are slightly smaller. The pelage is brown to brownish black on the back. There is long dense hair on the forehead and chins. In sexual mature males, the face is bluish gray in color.

Habits Inhabits mixed evergreen and deciduous forests and broad leaved forests at altitudes of 2000 m. They are gregarious, generally in small groups of 20 – 40 individuals, or in larger groups up to 50 – 70 individuals. The group is lead by a dominant adult male. It is diurnal, by night it sleeps in the top of trees, or sometimes sleeps on cliffs. Feeds mainly on plant matter, including tree leaves, seeds, and fruits, and also takes lizards and small birds.

Reproduction Mating peak occurs from September to October. Gestation lasts for about 6 months and the female usually delivers a single young from March to May, which she nurses for about 6 months. At one year the young is complete independent, but does not reach maturity until about 5 years of age. The life span is about 25 years.

Distribution Northern Sichuan, Shaanxi and southern Qinglin Mts. region.

Conservation China: II; CITES: appendix II.

Group of Chinese stump – tailed macaque

Macaca thibetana (♂)

Macaca thibetana (♀)

Pygathrix roxellanae
Chinese snub-nosed monkey

Description Head and body 52 – 78 cm, tail 57 – 80 cm, males weight about 17 kg and females about 8 kg. Rounded head, with short ears, the nose is turned upward. The face is sky blue in color. The dorsal coat of the males are covered with long, fine and dense golden hair about 30 cm in length. This coloration is not found in females.

Habits Inhabits mixed needle leaved and broad leaved forest and needle leafved forest at an altitudes of 1500 – 3500 m. They are arboreal and diurnal, rarely come down to the ground. The monkeys associate in groups of 100 – 200 individuals, or in smaller groups of 20 – 30 individuals. Feeds on tender leaves, young buds and inflorescence. Occasionally, in autumn they prey on young birds and insects.

Reproduction Mating peak period is from August to October and the births occur in March to May. The estrous cycle is 22 – 30 days, gestation is 193 – 203 days. Lactation period 5 – 6 month, normally have a single offspring. The age of sexual maturity in both sex is 4 – 6 years. The life span in captivity is 25 – 30 years.

Distribution Endemic species of China. Only found in Shaanxi, Sichuan, Gansu and Hubei with a population of 1000.

Conservation China: I; IUCN: VU; CITES: appendix I.

Pygathrix roxellanae

Pygathrix brelichi
Gray snub-nosed monkey

Description Head and body 64 – 69 cm, tail 70 – 85 cm, weight about 15 kg in male and female about 8 kg. The nose is flat. The body color is basically pale grayish brown; the face is grayish white or pale blue in color, the top of the head is grayish black. The grayish brown shoulders hair are long, with a length of 16 cm. The limbs are blackish brown. Tail dark gray at the base and is black or yellowish white at the tip. The newborn and young are silver gray in color.

Habits Inhabits broad leafed forest valleys, every green broad leafed forests and mixed forest of deciduous broad leafed and needle leafed forests at altitudes of 500 – 2000 m. They are diurnal and arboreal dwellers. Gather in large groups containing 50 – 100 individuals. At night they rest and sleep over 10 meters off the ground in high trees. Feeds mainly on leaves, buds, fruits and bark, also fond of insects and freshwater crabs.

Reproduction Mating occurs between summer and autumn with a peak mating period in September. The gestation period is 6 months, births take place in March and May. Usually gives birth to a single young. Sexual maturity is 3.5 – 4 years under captive conditions. It can mate with Chinese snub – nosed monkey and produce fertile hybrids.

Distribution Only found in Fan Jin Mts. of Guizhou. Estimated numbers of 900 – 1000 in the wild.

Conservation China: I; IUCN: EN; CITES: appendix I.

Pygathrix brelichi

PRIMATES

Pygathrix bieti
Black snub-nosed monkey

Description Head and body 74 – 83 cm, tail 51 – 72 cm. The shoulders of the males are overlaid with long grayish black hair. The calluses have long white hair, which form a conspicuous white patch on the rump. The tail hair is long and fluffy. The body coloration is similar in both sexes but the female has shorter hair. The face is blue, the nose turned upward, and the eyes are surrounded by a ring of white hair.

Habits Inhabit mixed broad leafed and needle leafed forests. Of the Chinese primates, this species live at the highest elevations 3500 – 4000m. This species is diumal and arboreal. Feeds mainly on fir and spruce needles. In the summer season their diet also includes young bamboo shoots and leaves and birch buds.

Reproduction Mating occurs from June to December, and the young are born from January to June. The gestation period is 189 – 198 days. The female usually gives birth to a single offspring.

Distribution An endemic species of China. It is found only in northwest Yunnan and southeast Xizang. The estimated population is 1000 – 1500 individuals in the wild.

Conservation China: I; IUCN: EN; CITES: appendix I.

Pygathrix bieti

Semnopithecus francoisi
François'leaf monkey

Description Body length about 52 – 71 cm, tail 70 – 90cm, and weight 6 – 9.5 kg. The head is small with a crested crown and it lacks cheek pouches. The color is uniformly black, but the head, neck and shoulders of the white-headed leaf monkey subspecies are, as indicated, white. The tail is black at the base and white at the tip. The color of the newborn and young are golden yellow, except the tail is grayish black.

Habits Inhabits limestone areas of subtropical and forest valleys. It is arboreal and diurnal. It is very agile, good at jumping and climbing, and can leap from tree to cliff with great ease. It lives in groups of 3 – 10 individuals, the group size does not exceed more than 20. Feeds on buds, young leaves, flowers, fruits and also insects.

Reproduction Mating occurs throughout the year, but peaks occur in autumn and winter. The estrous cycle is 24 (14 – 30) days, gestation lasts 6 – 7 months. The female delivers a single offspring once a year. Reach sexual maturity at 4 – 5 years.

Distribution Western Guangxi, southwestern and northern Guizhou with a population of 4000 – 6000 individuals in the wild.

Conservation China: I; IUCN: VU.

There are two other species in the Genus.
Semnopithecus pileatus
Capped leaf monkey

Distribution Northwest of Yunnan.
An estimated of 500 – 600 individuals.
Conservation China: I; IUCN: VU;
CITES: appendix 1.

Semnopithecus francoisi

Semnopithecus francoisi leucocephalus

Semnopithecus phayrei
Phayre's leaf monkey

Description Head and body length of males are 55 – 60 cm, tail 70 – 76cm, and weight 7.2 – 10.5 kg. The face is black, the skin around the eyes and mouth shows no trace of pigments; that region is ringed with a pale color. The crown is crested. The body color is silver gray or dark gray above; the thorax and belly are light gray, and the hands and feet are black.

Habits Inhabits tropical and monsoon rain forests and also in subtropical broad leafed evergreen forests. The leaf monkeys are diurnal and arboreal forest dwellers but may come down to the ground. The groups consist of 4 – 8 individuals. Feeds mainly on tender leaves, flower buds and fruits, but insects and birds' eggs are also eaten.

Distribution Southern Yunnan. An estimated of 12 000 – 17 000 surviving in the wild.

Conservation China: I; CITES; appendix II.

Semnopithecus phayrei （♀）

Semnopithecus phayrei（♂）

Semnopithecus entellus Hanuman langur

Description Head and body 62 – 79 cm, tail 67 – 93 cm, and weight 8 – 24 kg. The face is black, the body grayish brown above and the underparts paler. The cheeks hair and whiskers are long.

Habits Inhabits areas of subtropical montane forests. It is diurnal and arboreal. The langur spends most of its time on the ground in areas where woodland are scarce and sparse. Group sizes range from 12 to several dozen. Each group includes 2 adult males and several females.

Reproduction Mating occurs throughout the year. Births occur during April to May. The estrous cycle is about 30 days, gestation lasts 190 – 210 days. The langurs have an interbirth interval of 2 years. Litter size 1 – 2. The age at sexual maturity is 4 years in females and males 6 – 7 years. In captivity the life span is about 25 years.

Distribution Southeast parts of Xizang. Very rare.

Conservation China: I; CITES: appendix 1.

Party of group

Semnopithecus entellus

Mother with her young

PRIMATES

Hylobatidae

This family is the most specialized among the primates. The family is characterized by absence of the tail; the forelimbs are longer than the hindlimbs; they are arboreal dwellers; locomote brachially through the trees, and when on ground they walk on their hindlegs in an upright position. This family has 9 species and 4 species are distributed in China.

* *Hylobates concolor*
* *Hylobates hoolock*

* *Hylobates lar*
* *Hylobates leucogenys*

Hylobates hoolock Hoolock gibbon

Description Head and body 46 – 68 cm, there is no tail, and weight about 5.5 kg. Body slender, both sexes are similar in size. In males, the top of the head is black, the upper parts are blackish brown and the underparts are dull brown. The cheeks and lower jaw are white. The females are yellowish brown in color. The young grayish white and attain their final color several months later. The eyebrows of both sexes are white.

Habits Inhabits tropical forests of high mountainous regions. It is diurnal and arboreal. They travel by branchiation (alternately swinging the long arms), are rapid and agility in locomotion and can leap from tree to tree for a distance of more than 10 meters. The family group contains 3 – 5 individuals. Spacing calls of groups and individuals are frequently used. Feeds on leaves, various kinds of fruits, spiders, insects, small birds and eggs.

Reproduction Mating occurs during the rainy season. The estrous cycle is about 28 days, the gestation period is 7 – 7.5 months. The young are born from November through March.

Distribution Western parts of Yunnan. A small population about 200 individuals exist in the wild.

Conservation China: I; CITES: appendix 1.

Hylobates hoolock

The gibbon is about to swing

PRIMATES

Hylobates concolor Black gibbon

Description Head and body 45 – 63 cm. No tail, and weight about 6 kg. The body is slender, the forearms are longer than the hinglimbs. There is a long erect tuft of hairs on the head. The young gibbons are grayish yellow in color, when the males reach sexual maturity become entirely black color and the females are grayish brown to pale yellow.

Habits Inhabits tropical rain forests and natural woodlands at an altitude of 2000 m. They are highly arboreal forest dwellers and cannot live without the forest. The usual family group sizes range from 3 – 5 to 7 – 8 individuals. Feeds on berries, tenders leaves, bees and small animals.

Reproduction The gestation period is 7.5 months, sexual maturity at age of 7 – 8 years. The females produce one young and the interbirth interval is 2 – 3 years. The life span is 20 – 30 years.

Distribution Guangxi, Hainan and southern Yunnan. About 400 – 500 individuals in the wild.

Conservation China: I; IUCN: EN; CITES: appendix I.

Hylobales leucogenys
White-cheeked gibbon

Description Head and body 75 – 90 cm, there is no tail, and weight about 10.5 kg. The coat of the males is black, with white or yellowish white cheeks, the females is entirely yellowish white including the cheeks. Both sexes have a black crest on the top of the head.

Habits Inhabits throughout tropical rain forests and natural woods at an altitude of 1000 m. The habits of this species are similar to the Crested gibbon in most aspects.

Reproduction Similar to the Crested gibbon.

Distribution South Yunnan. About 70 – 80 individuals in the wild.

Conservation China I; CITES appendix I.

Hylobates concolor (Male at right with female black gibbon)

Hylobales leucogenys

PRIMATES

Hylobates lar White handed gibbon

Description Head and body 42 – 58 cm, no tail, and weight about 5.5 kg. The forelimbs are longer than the hindlimbs. The general coloration is black or grayish yellow, with white face. The hands and feet are white. The ischial callosities are small.

Habits Inhabit tropical rain forests at altitudes of 1 000 m. It is arboreal and diurnal. They move primarily by branchiation, using their arms and swinging their body forward through the trees. A single swing may cover a distance of 5 meters. The white handed gibbons can also climb vertical trees and run along slanted trees. On the ground they are able to walk upright, when in rapid locomotion they are capable of a quadrupedal motion. The gibbons are active by day and sleeps in trees at night. The usual family group size is 4 – 6 individuals, including 2 adults plus young and juveniles. Feeds mainly on leaves, tender twigs, flowers, fruits and insects and many other kinds of animal food.

Reproduction The estrous cycle is 30(21 – 43) days, the gestation period is 7 – 7.5 months. Produce one offspring with an interbirth interval of 2 to 2.5 years. Weaning is completed at 20 months. Under captive conditions it can live for 32 years.

Distribution Southern Yunnan. Estimated numbers only 30 – 40 individuals in the wild.

Conservation China: I; CITES: appendix 1.

Hylobates lar

CARNIVORA

The order Carnivora is characterized by a highly predatory nature, except for those few which prefer vegetative matter such as the lesser panda and the giant panda; They are adapted for predation, most species have highly developed canine teeth for stabbing and carnassials for sharing and cutting the flesh; Some species also have well developed soles and claws, such as feline; Some species have well developed limbs adapted for running, such as the wolf and cuon; Some species have long and slender bodies that are adapted to chase and catch prey in grasslands and shrub lands or enter burrows to hunt rodents such as the weasels and civets. There are 9 families and 235 species in the world, of these there are 7 families and 55 species in China.

Canidae	6	species
Ursidae	4	species
Ailuruidae	1	species
Mustelidae	20	species
Viverridae	10	species
Herpstidae	2	species
Felidae	12	species

Canidae

A small to medium sized carnivore with a body weight from 30 – 80 kg. The males usually are larger than the females. In the canidae family the Corsac fox is the smallest and the gray wolf is the largest. Canids have long and slender limbs. There are 5 digits on the forefoot and 4 digits on the hindfoot. The soles are small and the claws are blunt, unable to retract. The ears are large and erect. The tail is long and bushy. All species have anus and scent glands. Males have a well developed baculum. They are active throughout the year. The senses of smell, hearing and sight are very acute. They are good runners. There are 14 genera and 36 species in the world, of these China has 4 genera and 6 species.

* Canis lupus
* Vulpes corsac
* Vulpes ferrilata
* Vulpes vulpes
* Nyctereutes procyonoides
* Cuon alpinus.

Canis lupus Wolf

Description Head and body 100 – 150 cm, tail 31 – 51 cm, and weight 28 – 40 kg. The males are larger than the females. The ears are elect, the tail hangs down and is unable to rise. The coloration of the pelage is variable, but is generally grayish yellow or bluish gray.

Habits Inhabits forests, grasslands, tundra, steppes, semi – deserts, hilly land. Wolves do not have dens until the breeding period at which time the den is employed for the rearing of young. The same den may be used for several years. Most active in the night. It lives in packs or in family groups of 5 – 8 individuals. Feeds mainly on deer, but also on small animals such as rabbits, hares, and marmots.

Reproduction Mating occurs in early spring. The gestation period is 60 – 63 days and the young are born in late spring. The mean litter size is 6 (2 – 11) and are weaned about 6 – 8 weeks old. Sexual maturity 2 years of age.

Distribution In the past the wolves were distributed throughout the country but now have been eliminated from most parts of the country.

Conservation CITES: appendix II.

Canis lupus

Vulpes Vulpes Red fox

Description Head and body 45.5 – 90 cm, tail 35 – 55.5 cm, and weight about 7 kg. The ears are pointed and elect. The tail is long and bushy. The pelage color ranges from pale reddish brown to dark brown.

Habits Inhabit in a variety of habitats. The red fox lives solitarily before reproduction. Most active in the evening and night. Feeds mostly on rabbits, rodents and other small mammals as well as birds, frogs, snakes, insects, berries and vegetable matter.

Reproduction Mating occurs from late December to late March. The estrus cycle is 1 – 6 days and has a gestation period of 51 – 53 days. The young are born from March to May, litter size 1 – 10, occasionally up to 13. The young are weaned at 8 – 10 weeks of age, and reach sexual maturity at 10 months of age. Life span is 12 years.

Distribution Distribute throughout China.

Vulpes vulpes

Red fox in winter pelage

Head of a fox

Vulpes corsac `Corsac fox`

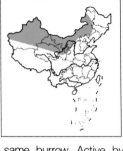

Description Head and body 50 – 60 cm, tail 25 – 35 cm, and weight 2 – 3 kg. The legs are relatively short, the ears are pointed, large and broad at the base. The color of upper parts are pale brownish gray or pale reddish brown, and the underparts pale white or pale yellow.

Habits Inhabits open steppes and semi deserts and does not live in forests. At times several individuals live together in the same burrow. Active by night. Feeds chiefly on rodents, and also birds, insects and lizards.

Reproduction Mating occurs from January to March. Gestation lasts 50 – 60 days, young are born in late spring and early summer. Females produce 1 litter per year and litter size 3 – 6 pups, sexual maturity is attained at the age of 2.

Distribution North China and northwest China.

vulpes ferrilata `Tibetan fox`

Description Head and body 57.5 – 70 cm, tail 24 – 29 cm, and weight about 7 kg. The coat is thick and soft and the tail is bushy. The color of the above are pale gray or pale reddish brown and white below. The tip of the tail is white.

Habits Inhabits mountain meadows and barren slops at altitudes of 1450 – 4800m. Most active in the morning and in the evening but sometimes in the day. Feeds on rodents, lagomorphs and ground birds.

Reproduction Mating occurs in late February. The young are born in April to May. Litter size 2 – 5.

Distribution Qingzang plateau.

Vulpes corsac

Vulpes ferrilata

Nyctereutes procyonoides Raccoon-dog

Description Head and body 50 – 60 cm, tail 13 – 25 cm, and weight 4 – 6 kg. The body is stocky, the legs and tail are relatively short. The pelage is long and bushy, dark brown and yellowish in color. The guard hair tips are black, which give an appearance of dull yellowish brown color, pale beneath.

Habits Inhabits open broad leafed forests near water, seldom found in dense forests of high mountains. It is nocturnal and solitary, but sometimes it lives in temporal family groups. It is omnivorous. Feeds mainly on rodents, fish, frogs, and other small animals, and vegetable matter, such as fruits, rhizomes, grains. It hibernates in the northern parts of the country.

Reproduction Mating begins in February to March. The gestation period is 59 – 64 days. There are 5 – 8 young per litter, but sometimes as many as 12. The weaning period is 2 months and the young are sexual maturity at 9 – 11 months of age. Life span 10 years.

Distribution Eastern China.

Cuon alpinus Dhole

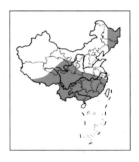

Description Head and body 88 – 113 cm, tail 40 – 50 cm, and weight 15 – 21 kg in males and the females 10 – 17 kg. The pelage is dark brown to reddish brown. The tail is long and bushy with a blackish brown tip.

Habits Inhabits mountainous forests. It is most active in the early morning and evening, but often active by day. The dhole lives in packs of 5 – 12 individuals and hunts in packs. Feeds mainly on wild pigs, muntjacs and on other cervidae and bovidae species.

Reproduction Mating occurs in winter. The gestation period is 60 – 62 days, births occur in spring with 4 – 6 cubs in a litter and are sexually mature in 1 year. In captivity the life span is 15 – 16 years.

Distribution Northeast and southern China. Rare in most regions.

Conservation China II; IUCN: VU; CITES: appendix II.

Nyctereutes procyonoides

Cuon alpinus

75

Ursidae

Large sized carnivore. Head and body length 100 – 280 cm with a short tail and weigh 27 – 800 kg, The males are larger than the females. The pelage is long and coarse, generally black, white or brown in color. The body is heavily built with short and strong limbs. The eyes are small, the ears are small and rounded. According to recent research the giant panda are closely related to the bears and are now put in the family ursidae. There are 7 genera and 8 species in the world. China has 4 genera and 4 species.

* *ursus thibetanus*
* *Ursus arctos*

* *Ursus malayanus*
* *Ailuropoda malanoleuca*

Ursus malayanus Sun bear

Description Head and body 100 – 140 cm, tail only 3 – 7 cm, shoulder height 70 cm, and weight 27 – 65 kg. This species is the smallest bear of the family Ursidae. The coat is black and there is a white or yellow V shape chest mark. But this feature is variable and lacking in some individuals.

Habits Inhabits tropical dense primeval forested regions of South Asia. It is a agile climber and is active at night, sleeps and baths in sun by day in trees at a height of 2 – 7 meters. The species does not hibernate. The diet is omnivorous. Feeds on larvae of wild bees, honey, termites, small vertebrates, berries and plant matter.

Reproduction The actual gestation period is about 95 days, but because of delay of implantation, the gestation may last up to 240 days. Litter size 1 – 2, the newborn weigh about 300 g. The life span under captive conditions was 24 years and 9 months.

Distribution Southern Yunnan, Numbers rare.

Conservation China: I; CITES: appendix I.

Ursus malayanus

Ursus thibetanus Asiatic black bear

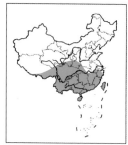

Description Head and body 120 – 180 cm, tail 6.5 – 16 cm. The males weight 110 – 250 kg and the females 65 – 125 kg. The legs are relatively short and stocky. The metatarsus and soles of the feet are large, the claws are strong and curved. The pelage is black with a white crescent on the chest.

Habits Inhabits broad leafed forests or mixed forests. They are found from hill lands to elevations as high as 2000 – 3000 m. Their sense of hearing is excellent but their sight is rather poor. They are solitary and active at night. They are omnivorous. Feeds mainly on young leaves, grass, fruits and a wide variety of seeds and are able to climb trees to obtain fruits. The diet also includes insects, small vertebrates and are fond of honey. They hibernate in winter.

Reproduction Mating occurs in June to July. The gestation period is 7 – 8 months. Births takes place in February, with 2 cubs in a litter and weaned at 3.5 months. Sexually mature at about 3 years. The life span in captivity is as long as 33 years.

Distribution Throughout the country in broad leafed forests or mixed needle and broad leafed forests regions.

Conservation China II; IUCN: VU; CITES: appendix I.

Ursus thibetanus

Ursus arctos Brown bear

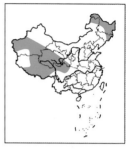

Description Head and body 170 – 210 cm, tail 6 – 21 cm, and weight 140 – 450 kg. It is a large sized bear. Have a hump over the shoulders. The pelage is yellowish brown to blackish brown. Usually the chest has no markings.

Habits Inhabits a variety type of forests. It lives on the ground, and is a poor climbers. The gait is a slow walk, but is capable of moving very fast. It has excellent senses of hearing and smell, but relatively poor eyesight. Active by day and night. Hibernation begins from October to December and ends from March to May. The diet is omnivorous. Feeds on roots, grasses, berries, and carcasses of animals. It occasionally kills young calves of moose, red deer and black bear. It may also catch fish when available.

Reproduction Mating takes place from may to July, and gives birth in February to March after 180 – 226 days of gestation. Litter size 2(2 – 4), the cubs are naked and blind, weigh 340 – 680 g. The cubs are weaned at about 5 months of age. They are sexually mature at 4 – 6 years. Longevity in captivity as great as 50 years, and in the wild under natural conditions may live for 25 years.

Distribution Northeast, northwest and southwest China.

Conservation China: II; CITES: appendix I.

Ursus arctos

Hind foot (left) and head of the Brown bear (right)

Mother and cubs

CARNIVORA

Ailuropoda melanoleuea Giant panda

Description Head and body 1.5 – 1.8 m in adult males, shoulder height 65 – 70 cm, tail 12 – 14 cm, and weight 80 – 125kg. The females are 10% – 20% smaller than the males. The head is round, body stocky with a short tail. The eyes, ears, shoulders and limbs are dark black and the rest of the body is milky white.

Habits Inhabits high montane forests at altitudes of 1300 – 1600 m. It is frequently found in undergrowth of mixed coniferous and broad leafed forests with square and arrow bamboo or other types of bamboo stands. It is solitary, except for females and their young. It can swim and is a good climber. Feeds mainly on bamboo stems and shoots, and fruits of plant matter such as Kiwi fruit (Actinida chinensis) and sometimes on carcasses of small mammals.

Reproduction Mating occurs from March to May. The estrus period is 1 – 3 days, gestation ranges from 112 – 163 days, this is because panda exist 1.5 – 4 months of delay in implantation, the actual embryonic development is about 1.5 months. The females produce 1 young per litter, occasionally 2. The young weigh 90 – 130 g at birth, takes bamboo at 5 – 6 months of age, and are weaned at about 8 – 9 months. They may remain with their mother about 18 months. Sexual maturity is around 5.5 – 6 years of age. Interval between birth is 2 years. Longevity in captivity is 26 years.

Distribution Sichuan, Gansu and Shaanxi.

Conservation China: I; IUCN: EN; CITES; appendix I.

The habitat of Giant panda

3 day after birth (above) and at age of 26 days (below)

82

Ailuropodo melanoleuea

83

Giant panda climbs high up in a tree

Lying and resting

CARNIVORA

Ailuruidae

There is only a single species

Ailurus fulgens Lesser panda

Description Head and body 51 – 73 cm, tail 40 – 49 cm, and weight 4.5 – 6 kg. The head is short and wide with a rather round face. The limbs are short and the feet have 5 toes with retractile claws. The tail is long, bushy and banded with 9 rust brown and sandy yellow rings. The pelage is brown.

Habits Inhabits high subtropical mountain forests of broad leafed or mixed broad

leafed and coniferous forest at altitudes of 1400 – 4000 m. It is active from dusk to dawn, and small groups of 2 – 5 are formed. It can rapidly climb high trees and move through trees when a threats appears. The diet is omnivorous. Feeds mainly on arrow bamboo or other kinds of bamboo shoots and leaves or tender leaves of plants, and sometimes insects, and carcasses of animals.

Reproduction Mating occurs in February and March. Births takes place from June to July. The gestation period is 120 – 150 days. Females produce I litter annually of 1 – 3 young, usually 1 or 2. The young stay with the mother for about 1 year. In captivity it may live 13 years and 5 months.

Distribution Yunnan and Sichuan. Very rare.

Conservation China II; IUCN: EN; CITES: appendix II.

Head of the Lesser panda

Walk on the ground

Ailurus fulgens

CARNIVORA

Mustelidae

Mustelidae have elongate bodies, or heavily built bodies. The smallest species is the least weasels, which has a weight as low as 25 g. The largest species is the wolverine, which the body weight reaches 25 kg. Usually males are larger than females. The legs are short, the claws are non-retractile. The ears are short and rounded. Most of the species have well developed anal glands. There are 23 genera and 64 species, of these 9 genera and 20 species occur in China.

* *Mustela altaica*
* *Mustela erminea*
* *Mustela eversmanni*
  Mustela amurensis
  Mustela kathiah
* *Mustela nivalis*
* *Mustela sibirica*
  Mustela strigidorsa
  Vormela peregusna
* *Martes flavigula*

* *Martes zibellina*
* *Martes foina*
* *Gulo gulo*
* *Meles meles*
* *Arctonyx collaris*
* *Melogale moschata*
  Melogale personata
* *Lutra lutra*
  Lutra perspicillata
* *Aonyx cinerea*

Mustela sibirica Siberian weasel

Description Head and body 34 – 40 cm, tail 12 – 25 cm, weight 330 – 1200 g in males, females about 210 – 550 g. They have long slender bodies with short legs. Tail very bushy in winter. Body coloration yellowish to tan brown.

Habits Inhabits open cultivated lands near water net works. Builds its nest in hollow of trees, among rock piles, mud heaps and also in hay stacks or in old buildings. Active at evening and morning, but also active during day when the vegetation is dense. Feeds mostly on small rodents, amphibians, but also birds, fish and other invertebrates.

Reproduction Mating occurs in March to April. Gestation period is 33 – 37 days. Born in late May, usually 5 – 6 individuals per litter, occasionally as many as 12. The young weigh 5 – 7 g at birth and are weaned at 5 – 6 weeks of age. Sexual maturity at 9 – 10 months of age.

Distribution Throughout China, except in deserts and loess plateau regions.

Mustela sibirica (above), 7 days old (left), Head (right)

Mustela nivalis Least weasil

Description Head and body 14 – 21 cm, tail 3 – 7 cm, and weight 50 – 130. Males may reach a weight of 250 g, while females are smaller. In summer the pelage is brown above and white below. In winter its pelage entirely white, except the tail has brownish black tip.

Habits The habitat and activities are similar to the stoat, but prefers a drier environment. Active at night. Feeds mostly on small rodents, and is able to enter into burrows to kill prey.

Reproduction Females are polyestrous. Gestation period 35 – 37 days, gives birth to 1 – 3 litters in a year, with 5(3 – 10) young per litter. The young are sexually mature at 4 months of age.

Distribution Northeast, northwest and south west China. Rare.

Mustela altaica Alpine weasel

Description Head and body 22.4 – 28.7 cm, tail 10.8 – 14.5 cm, and weight 217 – 350 g in males. Female weigh 122 – 220 g. The pelage is short, yellowish brown or brownish yellow above, the underparts pale yellow or orange yellow. The tail is not bushy.

Habits Inhabits steppes, meadows, forests and plateaus up to an elevations of 3500 m. Dens in rock crevices, tree roots, or in rodent burrows. Active at night or at dawn and dust. Feeds mainly on ground squirrels, pikas and small birds.

Reproduction Mating occurs in February and March. Females gives birth to 2 – 8 young from early spring to late summer after 40 days of gestation. Reach sexual maturity at I year of age.

Distribution Northeast, northwest to southwest China.

Mustela nivalis

Mustela altaica

CARNIVORA

Mustela erminea Stoat

Description Head and body 17 – 32 cm, tail 4 – 12 cm and weight 42 – 260g. They have long slender bodies and short legs, the ears are small and covered by fur. The pelage on the back, and sides are brown and yellow on the undersides in summer, the tail end is black. The coat is snow white in winter except the black tail tip.

Habits Inhabits in a variety of habitats from open tundra to deep forest, plain areas, marsh lands and cultivated lands, especially near river valleys. The dens are under tree roots, in hollow logs, among rock crevices, under rocks, wood piles and old burrows of rodents. It is mainly nocturnal and solitary except during breeding season. It is a good climber and excellent swimmer. When in danger or been frightened, it emits an unpleasant odor from the anal glands. It is a strict carnivore. Feeds mainly on rodents such as ground squirrels, meadow mouse, hamsters and also small birds, reptiles, frogs, fish insects, and occasionally hares.

Reproduction Mating takes place in late spring to early summer, but the implantation of the fertilized eggs is delayed until the following February – March. The females give birth from March to April. Gestation lasts 10 months, but the embryonic development is actually about 1 month. Each litter has 3 – 9 individuals. Eyes open at 5 – 6 weeks, weaned at 6 weeks. At 8 weeks of age hunt with the mother. Males reach sexual maturity in 1 year and females reach sexual maturity at an age of 2 – 3 months and can mate in their first summer.

Distribution Northeast and Xizang. Very rare.

Mustela erminea (in winter pelage)

Mustela erminea (in summer pelage)

Mustela eversmanni Steppe polecat

Description Head and body 37 – 56 cm, tail 11 – 15 cm and weight 700 – 1000 g in males, females weigh only 500 g. The mid back has especially long hairs. Pelage brownish yellow or sandy yellow on upper parts and somewhat darker at the hind half. There are brownish black markings between and around the eyes.

Habits Inhabits open grassland and semi-desert. It is nocturnal and solitary and lives in burrows. The sense of smell and hearing are acute. Feeds mostly on pikas, ground squirrels, hamsters, marmots, and other rodents. It also eats fish and frogs.

Reproduction Mating occurs from January to March. Gestation lasts 38 – 41 days, births take place in April – May. Litter size 4 – 10 young, weigh 4 – 6 g at birth and sexual maturity at 9 months of age.

Distribution Northern Sichuan and north of the Yellow River basin.

Mustela eversmanni

Some other species of Mustela:

Mustela amurensis Amur polecat

Brief description Smaller than least steppe polecat, weigh 300 – 600 g. Inhabits forest edge, steppes and cultivated lands. Habits are similar to the Steppe polecat.

Distribution Lesser Hinggan Lin Mts. and in grasslands areas of Northeast China.

Mustela kathiah Yellow-bellied weasel

Brief description Body weight about 200g. Pelage color yellowish brown above and bright yellow below. Inhabits subtropical forest.

Distribution Southern China. Rare.

Mustela strigidorsa Back-stripped weasel

Brief description The size and coloration are similar to the Yellow-bellied weasel, but there is a white stripe, which runs along the back.

Habits Inhabits evergreen broad forest.

Distribution Southwest montane forests.

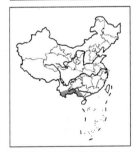

Vormela peregusna Marbled polecat

Description Body weight 370 – 700 g. The color of the back pale yellow, with a mixture of brown stripes.

Habits Inhabits desert steppes. Feeds on rodents.

Distribution Deserts of northern China.

Martes zibellina Sable

Description Head and body of males 39 cm, tail 13 cm, and weight 880 – 910 g, females weigh 760 – 780. The body is slender with short legs. The ears are large, erect and slightly round at the tip. The tail is bushy. The coat is dark brown to grayish brown, with a orangish yellow or a white patch on the throat.

Habits Inhabits subcold coniferous forest zones of Mount Altai and Great Hinggan Lin Mts. mixed broad leafed and coniferous forests of Mount Chanbaishan and Lesser Hinggan Lin Mts. It is solitary, chiefly nocturnal and terrestrial, but climbs trees easily. Dens are found among rocks, logs, burrows under trees. Feeds mainly on small mammals, forest birds, and also eats nuts and vegetable matter such as berries.

Reproduction Mating takes place from June to August. Births occur in the second year in February or March. Gestation lasts 250 – 300 days, this is because of delayed implantation of about 10 months, but the actual embryonic development takes about 25 – 40 days. Litter size 1 – 5 individuals, usually 3 – 4. Weaned at 7 weeks of age and reach sexual maturity at 15 – 16 months. Captive life span is 15 years.

Distribution Northeast China and northern XinJiang forested areas.

Conservation China: I.

Martes zibellina

Sable cubs

97

Martes flavigula
Yellow-throated marten

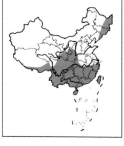

Distribution Head and body 45 – 65 cm, tail 37 – 45 cm, and weight 2 – 3 kg. The ears are short and rounded, the tail is not bushy. The pelage is brown to blackish brown. There is a bright yellow patch on the throat and breast.

Habits Inhabits a variety of forests. The nest sites are found in tree holes or in rock crevices. It is active at dawn and dust, but often hunts during the day. Feeds mainly on rodents and other small animals, but nuts are also consumed. Occasionally it preys on young ungulates such as muntjac and musk deer. It is fond of honey.

Reproduction Mating occurs in June to July and gives birth in May of the following year with 2 – 4 young. Gestation period（including delayed implantation）9 – 10 months. Captive individuals may live up to 14 years.

Distribution Found throughout forested areas. The numbers are rare.

Conservation China：II.

Martes foina Stone marten

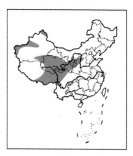

Distribution Head and body 40 – 50 cm, tail 22 – 30 cm, and weight 1.1 – 2.3 kg. Grayish brown to dull brown in color. The tail is bushy.

Habits Inhabits rocky forests, open steppes and areas of loess ravine. Nests are found in rock crevices and in hollow trees. Active at dawn and dust. Feeds on small vertebrates and also berries.

Reproduction Mating occurs in summer. Gestation lasts 230 – 275 days （including delayed implantation）, the female gives birth to 3 – 4 young per litter. May live up to 14 years in captivity.

Distribution Central and western China.

Conservation China：II.

Martes flavigula

Martes foina

99

Gulo gulo Wolverine

Description Head and body 65 – 105 cm, tail 17 – 26 cm, and weight 7 – 20 kg, males may reach up to 35 kg. Females are smaller than the males. Is has a stout muscular body, the legs are short with large bear – like paws. The pelage is long and dark brown.

Habits Inhabits boreal temperate forests. It is nocturnal and terrestrial and is a good swimmer and climber. Feeds on carrion or anything available in the habitat, it also takes berries.

Reproduction Mating occurs from September to November. Births take place in February and April. Gestation period 120 – 272 days (includes delayed implantation), the female gives birth to 2 – 4 young per year, which reach sexual maturity at 2 – 3 years. Life span 17 years.

Distribution Northern Xinjiang and Helongjiang. Rare.

Conservation China: I; IUCN: VU.

Melogale moschata
Chinese ferret badger

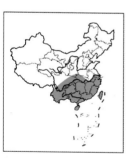

Description Head and body 35 – 43 cm, tail 15 – 23 cm, and weight 1.0 – 1.5 kg. Males and females are similar in size. The snout is long and the ears are short. There is a white patch on the forehead and a white stripe running along the back.

Habits Inhabits forest slops, forest edges, ravines or near cultivated lands, they avoid deep forest. Active at night. Feeds mainly on small animals, includes earthworms, insects, frogs, and rodents. The diet also consists 10% – 20% of plant material, such as tubers, rhizomes and fruits.

Reproduction Mating occurs in February to March. Born in April to May, with 2 – 4 young in a litter, which reach sexual maturity at 9 – 10 month of age.

Distribution South of Qinglin Mts. region.

Gulo gulo

Melogale moschata

Meles meles Eurasian badger

Description Head and body 50 – 60 cm, tail 15 – 19 cm, and weight 5 – 10 kg. In autumn it may reach up to 16 kg. The body is stocky, with short legs and powerful claws. The pelage is coarse, the tail blackish brown.

Habits Inhabits mainly in forest edges and in shrubs of mountain slops. It is nocturnal and gregarious. It lives in family groups in burrow systems. It is omnivorous. Feeds mainly on plant material such as roots, stems, fruits, and also on small animals or carrion.

Reproduction Mates in summer. Gestation lasts about 10 months and 2 – 6 young are born the following year. Reach sexual maturity in 1 year. The life span is 16 years in captivity.

Distribution Throughout China, except desert areas.

Arctonyx collaris Hog badger

Description Head and body 55 – 70 cm, tail 12 – 17 cm, and weight 6 – 14 kg. Size and coloration are similar to the Eurasian badger, but the snout is much long and ends like a pig's snout. The tail is white.

Habits Inhabits forests, shrubs, and in a variety of habitats up to altitudes of 3500 m. It is solitary, nocturnal and omnivorous. Feeds mainly on roots, stems, fruits, earthworms, insects, fish, frogs, rodents and carrion. It hibernates in the winter.

Reproduction Mating occurs from April to September. Female gives birth in April and May. Gestation lasts about 10 months, but true gestation is less than 6 weeks. Captive hog badgers have lived for 14 years.

Distribution Throughout south of Yellow River basin, especially in the south part of Yangzi River.

Meles meles

Arctonyx collaris

Lutra lutra Eurasian otter

Description Head and body 55 – 70 cm, tail 30 – 50 cm, and weight 3 – 7.5 kg. The feet are webbed, the claws are short and sharp. The coat is dense, dark chocolate above and paler below.

Habits Inhabits rivers, lakes, streams, reservoirs, along coastline and islands. It is solitary, shelters in burrows at day and is active at night. Feeds chiefly on fish.

Reproduction Reproduces throughout the year, but mainly in August. Gestation lasts 55 – 63 days, with 1 – 5 young per litter, usually 2. Sexually mature at 2 – 3 years of age and the longevity in captivity is about 15 years.

Distribution Water areas and coastal islands.

Conservation China: II; CITES: appendix II.

Aonys cinerea
Oriental small-clawed otter

Description Head and body 42 – 54 cm, tail 23 – 33 cm, and weight 2.7 – 5.4 kg. The claws are small and do not extend to the toes. The feet are webbed. The body color is brown above and grayish white beneath.

Habits Inhabits rivers, small streams, and coastal areas of estuaries. It lives in groups of up to 10 individuals. Feeds mainly on fish, mollusks and large crustaceans.

Reproduction Estrous cycle is 24 – 30 days, the gestation period is 60 – 64 days. Produces 1 – 2 litters a year, each with 1 – 6 young, usually 2. The young are sexual maturity at 1 year. The life span is 11 year in captivity.

Distribution Water areas of southern China and southern Xizang.

Conservation China: II; CITES: appendix II.

Lutra lutra

Aonys cinerea

Viverridae

Viverridae are small and medium sized tropical and subtropical carnivores. The smallest species weigh less than 1 kg and the largest species weigh over 10 kg. The body is long and slim with short legs, the tail usually long. The ears are small and rounded. The body and the tail of most species have stripes and spots. The famous substance called "civet" is secreted from the well developed perianal glands, located at the perineum of the small Indian civet and large Indian civet cat. There are 18 genera and 35 species in the world and China has 9 genera and 10 species.

* *Viverricula indica*
  Viverra megaspila
* *Viverra zibetha*
* *Prionodon pardicolor*
* *Arctogalidea trivirgata*

* *Paradoxurus hermaphroditus*
* *Paguma larvata*
* *Arctictis binturong*
* *Chrotogale owstoni*
  Cynogale lowei

Viverra zibetha Large Indian civet

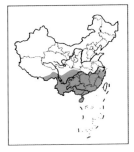

Description Head and body 67 – 83 cm, tail 40 – 51 cm, and weight 5 – 11 kg. The tail has black and white rings. There is a perianal gland located at the perineum.

Habits Inhabits forest edges, dense shrubs, and herbosa. The nocturnal and solitary civet has a wide variety of food. Feeds mainly on rodents, small animals, and also eats plant material.

Reproduction Mating occurs in spring. The gestation period is about 2 – 2.5 months, young are born in late spring and early summer, weaned at 3 – 4 months. Litter size 2 – 4. The life span is about 10 years.

Distribution South of Yangzi River.

Conservation China: II.

Viverra zibetha

Viverricula indica Small indian civet

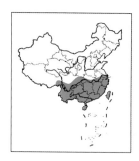

Description Head and body 45 – 63 cm, tail 30 – 43 cm, and weight 2 – 4 kg. The tail is long and slender, somewhat thick at the base and tapers down to the tip. The body color is brownish yellow. The legs and feet are dark brown. There are 5 continuous or incomplete blackish brown stripes or spots running lengthwise on the back. The tail is brownish yellow, and has 6 – 8 brownish black tail rings.

Habits Inhabits hilly lands, bunchshrubs, or cultivated lands. It is both solitary and terrestrial, it seldom climbs trees. Active at night, especially at dusk. It has a habit of rubbing its scent on small stones, small trees or various objects while moving along the trailside. Feeds on a variety of foods, mainly on rodents, insects, fish and frogs. It also eats berries.

Reproduction Mating occurs in spring season. Gives birth in May to June. The number of young per litter is 4 – 5, reach sexually mature the following year. Life span in captivity is about 10 years.

Distribution South of Yangzi River.

Conservation China: II.

Paguma larvata Masked palm civet

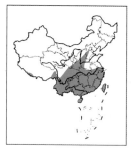

Description Head and body 51 – 76 cm, tail 51 – 64 cm, and weight 3.6 – 5.0 kg. Body color greenish gray, the limbs pale blackish brown. The face is white, around the eyes and on the chin is a distinctive black facial mask.

Habits Inhabits forests. It is nocturnal and dwells in burrows. Lives in small family groups of a few individuals to more than 10 individuals, except when they pair off during the breeding season. Feeds on a variety of fruits, but also rodents, frogs, snakes and small animals.

Reproduction Mating peaks in February and March but may extend into August. Gives birth mainly in August. The gestation period is 70 – 90 days, and litter size 1 – 5 young, usually 2 – 3. The young reach sexually mature at 1 year of age. Captive individuals may live up to 15 years.

Distribution From south of Hebei and Shanxi to Taiwan and Hainan.

Viverricula indica

Paguma larvata

109

CARNIVORA

Prionodon pardicolor Spotted linsang

Description Head and body 35 – 40 cm, tail 30 – 36 cm, and weight less than 1000g. Small with long and slender body. The fur is short, soft and dense. The over all color is grayish brown or orangish yellow, but there are dark black spots along the back and sides. Tail has 8 – 10 black rings.

Habits Inhabits evergreen broad leafed forests, shrubs, at edge of forests and tall grass of subtropical areas. It is nocturnal. The senses of smell and hearing are well developed. Feeds mainly on small rodents, frogs, lizards, insects and also takes berries.

Reproduction Mating begins in late spring. There are 2 young per litter. The life span in captivity is about 7 – 8 years.

Distribution Guizhou, Huinan, and south of Jiangxi. The population is low.

Conservation China: II; CITES: appendix I.

Paradoxurus hermaphroditus
Common palm civet

Description Head and body 50 – 60 cm, tail length as long as the head and body, and weight 2.4 – 4 kg. The fur is pale brown with 3 – 5 dark stripes or spots from neck to the back. The tail is long, brownish black with no rings.

Habits Inhabits montane forests. It is nocturnal, solitary, arboreal and omnivorous. Spends most of its time on trees, seldom comes to the ground. Feeds on rodents, small birds and other small animals and also berries.

Reproduction Breeds throughout the year. Young have been found from October to December. Litters contain 2 – 4 young and reach sexual maturity at 11 – 12 months. Captive individuals have lived for 22 years.

Distribution Yunnan, Guangdong, Guangxi and Hainan.

Prionodon pardicolor

Paradoxurus hermaphroditus

111

Chrotogale owstoni
Owston's palm civet

Description Head and body 51 – 64 cm, tail 31 – 48 cm. Body long and slender, the snout is elongated. The back has 4 large black transverse bands, which extend to the body sides. The tail is black and at the base of the tail has 2 whitish rings.

Habits Inhabits tropical rain forests and near streams of sparse bunchshrubs. It is solitary and nocturnal, and forages on the ground. Feeds mainly on earthworms and other small animals.

Distribution Eastern Yunnan, and southern Guangxi.

Conservation IUCN: VU.

Arctogalidia trivirgata
Small-toothed palm civet

Description Head and body 43 – 53 cm, tail 51 – 60 cm, and weight 2 – 2.5 kg. The tail is longer than the head and body length. The back, tail and outer sides of the 4 limbs are grayish brown, the head is darker. There is a white stripe on the nose and 3 brown or black stripes running lengthwise down the back. The median stripe is distinct and complete, but the lateral stripes are discontinued, alternating with broken spots or absent. There is a white patch on the breast.

Habits Inhabits tropical rain forests at altitudes below 500 meters. It is arboreal, active at night and rests at day in high branches of tall trees. Feeds on all kinds of animals and fruits.

Reproduction Breeds throughout the year. Two litters per year, each litter contains 2 – 3 young. Gestation lasts 45 days, weaned at about 2 months. Captive individuals may live about 15 years.

Distribution South of Yunnan.

Chrotogale owstoni

Arctogalidia trivirgata

Arctictis binturong Binturong

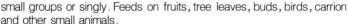

Description Head and body 61 – 96. 5 cm, tail 56 – 89 cm, and weight 9 – 14 kg. The fur is long, coarse, black and lustrous. The ears have long hairs on the back. The tail has a prehensile tip.

Habits Inhabits tropical rain forests. It is nocturnal and arboreal, seldom descends to the ground. By day its sleeps and rests among the branches of tall trees. It lives in small groups or singly. Feeds on fruits, tree leaves, buds, birds, carrion and other small animals.

Reproduction Breeding continuous throughout the year. The estrous cycle averages 82 days, gestation lasts 84 – 99 days. Litters contain 1 – 6 young and sexual maturity is attained at the age of 28 – 30 months. Captive individuals may live for 22 years and 8 months.

Distribution Southwest of Yunnan.

Conservation China: I.

There are two other species in the family that are given briefly.

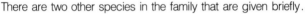

Viverra megaspila Large-spotted civet

Brief description Head and body 75 – 95 cm, tail 30 – 37 cm, weight 8 – 9 kg. There are large dark marked spots along the sides. One litter per year. Litter size 1 – 3.

Distribution Southwest Yunnan. Rare in number.

Cynogale lowei Tonkin otter-civet

Brief description Head and body 57 – 67 cm, tail 12 – 20 cm, weight 3 – 5 kg. The pelage is short, coarse, and gray in color. The whiskers are very long. Semi – aqautic. Feeds on crustaceans, mollusks, fish, birds, and small invertebrates and also berries.

Distribution Red River Valley of southern Yunnan.

Binturong head

Arctictis binturong

Herpstidae

Small carnivores of tropical and subtropical regions. The body weight is usually less than 3 kg. The tail is thick and large at the base and gradually tapers toward the tip. The guard hairs are long, coarse and bushy. Their are no distinctive stripes or spots on the body. There are 18 genera and 39 species, of these China has only 1 genus and 2 species.

     * *Herpestes javanicus*   * *Herpestes urva*

Herpestes javanicus
Small Asian mongoose

Description Head and body 25 – 35 cm, tail about 25 cm, and weight 0.6 – 1.0 kg. Shape similar to the Crab-eating mongoose. The body color is brownish gray, around the eyes, cheeks and chin are brownish red.

Habits Inhabits hilly lands, shrublands, cultivated lands and mixed wood stands near streams of South Asia tropical areas. Active at day. Feeds on rodents, frogs, and insects.

Reproduction Annually 1 litter with 2 – 4 young. The gestation period lasts about 7 weeks.

Distribution Yunnan, Guangxi and Hainan.

Herpestes urva Crab-eating mongoose

Description Head and body 36 – 52 cm, tail 17 – 26 cm, and weight 1 – 2.3 kg. The guard hairs are coarse, hard and bushy. Body is sandy brown, the tail is about the same color.

Habits Inhabits mountain ravines, forest streams. It is terrestrial, good at swimming, but not a good climber. Active at dawn and dust, lives either alone or in pairs. Feeds on frogs, loachs, snails, crabs and small invertebrates.

Reproduction Mating occurs in spring. The gestation period is 50 to 60 days and the female delivers 2 – 4 young.

Distribution South of Yangzi River.

Herpestes javanicus

Herpestes urva

117

CARNIVORA

Felidae

The body size of the cat family is quite distinct has a range of 1.5 – 306 kg. Males are larger than females. In most species the limbs are strong with sharp, curved and retractile claws. The incisors are small, the canines are long and sharp, the carnassials are well developed which are adapted to cutting the food. The surface of the tongue is covered with sharp horny papillae, which are used for taking the flesh off the bone. The felids are found in a large variety of habitats, except for polar and tundra areas. They are terrestrials and most species are solitary, many are nocturnal. They have excellent senses of hearing and sight. There are 5 genera and 36 species, of these China has 4 genera and 12 species.

* *Felis bengalensis*
* *Felis bieti*
  Felis chaus
* *Felis manul*
* *Felis marmorata*
* *Felis silvestris*

* *Felis temmincki*
* *Lynx lynx*
* *Neofelis nebulosa*
* *Panthera pardus*
* *Panthera tigris*
* *Panthera uncia*

Felis bieti Chinese desert cat

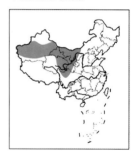

Description Head and body 68.5 – 85 cm, tail 29 – 35 cm, and weight about 5.5 kg. The ground color is grayish yellow, but the back is somewhat reddish. There are some long fine hairs scatter about the body. The underside of the body is white or pale gray. The cheeks have distinct transverse brown stripes. The back of the ears are black, and there are long tufts of hair up to 2 cm from the ears. The tail has black or dark color rings and a black tip.

Habits Inhabits deserts, semi-deserts, open steppes or sparse woodlands, shrublands and are found in high mountains up to altitudes of 3 000 m. They are active at night. Feeds mainly on rodents and preys on mountain birds, lizard and small vertebrates.

Reproduction Mating begins in winter. The gestation period is about 2 months, births occur in May, annually 1 litter.

Distribution Arid areas of north China and northwest China. It is an endemic species of China. Rare in number.

Conservation China: II; CITES: appendix II.

Felis bieti

CARNIVORA

Felis silvestris Forest wild cat

Description Head and body 50 – 70 cm, tail 21 – 35 cm, and weight 3 – 8 kg. Males are larger than females. The fur color is grayish yellow, with many irregular transverse brownish black spots on the body, the legs also have small spots. The tail has several dark rings.

Habits Inhabits a wide variety of forests, semi-deserts, open steppes, marsh and rocky areas. It is solitary and nocturnal, but active mainly at dawn and at dusk. Feeds mainly on rodents and other small vertebrates.

Reproduction Mating occurs in February and March, usually 1 litter per year. The gestation period lasts 63 – 68 days, 2 – 4 young are born, weaned at about 30 days and reach sexual maturity at 10 – 12 months of age.

Distribution Xinjiang, Gansu. Rare in number.

Conservation China: II; CITES appendix II.

Felis marmorata Marbled cat

Description Head and body 40 – 60 cm, tail 45 – 55 cm, and weight about 5.5 kg. The body is long and slender, the head is broad and rounded. The body color is grayish brown to yellowish brown. The back and sides of the body are marked with black margined irregular rosettes, and the rest of its body has small black spots. The ears are short, rounded, and black at the back. The tail is black at the tip.

Habits Inhabits tropical and subtropical forests. It is nocturnal and arboreal. Feeds on squirrels, flying squirrels, small rodents, and also prey on birds and lizards.

Distribution Southwest of Yunnan. Rare in number.

Conservation CITES: I.

Felis silvestris

Felis marmorata

A pelage of Forest wild cat

121

Felis bengalensis Leopard cat

Description Head and body 36 – 90 cm, tail 15 – 37 cm, and weight 3 – 8 kg. The back is yellowish brown or grayish brown and the whole body is covered with dark brown or pale brown spots. From the head to the shoulders there are 4 black stripes running lengthwise.

Habits Inhabits montane forests, grasslands, cultivated lands, residents areas and in many kinds of habitat. It is solitary, nocturnal and mainly terrestrial. It is an agile climber. Feeds chiefly on rodents, birds, hares and other small vertebrates.

Reproduction Mating occurs from January to February. The gestation period is 63 – 70 days, births take place in March and May, the females produce 2 – 4 young per litter, which reach sexual maturity at 18 months.

Distribution Throughout China, except in areas of plateau and desert.

Conservation CITES: appendix II.

Felis temmincki Asiatic golden cat

Description Head and body 73 – 105 cm, tail 43 – 56 cm, and weight 12 – 16 kg. The coat color varies from dark brown, reddish brown, grayish green or with a pattern of spots or stripes on the body. The ears are short and rounded, and the back of the ears are black.

Habits Inhabits a wide variety of forested habitats including high altitude forests. It is nocturnal, solitary and mainly terrestrial and a good climber. Feeds mainly on rodents and insectivores, and also birds, Indian muntjac, hares, and lizards.

Reproduction There is no confirmed breeding season. The gestation period is 91 days, and litters consist of 2 – 3 young, which weigh about 250 g at birth. The life span of the golden cat is about 18 years in captivity.

Distribution Southern China forested areas.

Conservation China: II; CITES: appendix I

Felis bengalensis   *Felis temmincki*

Felis temmincki

Felis manul Pallas'cat

Description Head and body 50 – 65 cm, tail 21 – 35 cm, and weight 2.3 – 3.5 kg. The body is bulky, the legs short and stocky. The head is short and broad with large eyes. The ears are short, bluntly, rounded, and wide apart. The pelage is long and dense, the back is sandy or grayish brown. There are a few small black spots on the head. The tail is thick with several subterminal rings, and has a black rounded tip.

Habits Inhabits steppes, deserts, plateaus, rocky mountain sides, up to altitudes of 3000 – 4000 m. It is solitary and nocturnal, but it is very active at dawn and dust. Feeds mainly on rodents, small mammals and birds.

Reproduction Mating occurs in February, and the females give birth to 3 – 6 kittens in April – May.

Distribution Northeast, and northwest China.

Conservation China: II; CITES: appendix II

Felis chaus Jungle cat

Description Head and body 60 – 76 cm, tail 25 – 29, weight 5 – 9 kg. There are long tufts of hair up to 1.5 cm on the ear tips. The tail is short, has 2 – 3 rings and ends in a black tip.

Habits Inhabits forests, open steppes and many kinds of environment. Feeds on hares and small animals.

Reproduction The female produces 2 – 5 kittens per litter. The young are mature sexually at 18 months of age.

Distribution Western China.

Conservation China: II; CITES: appendix II.

Felis manul

Pallas' cat in winter pelage

125

Lynx lynx Eurasian lynx

Description Head and body 80 – 13 cm, tail 11 – 24.5 cm, and weight 18 – 38 kg. There are long hairs on each side of the cheeks. The ears are tipped with long pensiles of hair up to 4 – 7 cm. The tail is short and has a black tip.

Habits Inhabits mountain forests, scrubs, dense forests and bare rocky areas. It is solitary. Feeds mainly on hares, birds, rodents and young deer.

Reproduction Mating occurs in spring. The gestation period is 63 – 74 days, usually with 2 – 3 kittens. The males reach sexual maturity at 21 months and the females at 33 months. Life span 17 – 22 years.

Distribution Northwest and northeast China. Rare in number.

Conservation China: II; CITES: appendix II.

Lynx lynx (in deserts)

Lynx lynx (in grassland)

Lynx eats a killed antelope

Neofelis nebulosa Clouded leopard

Description Head and body 61 – 106 cm, tail 55 – 91 cm, and weight 16 – 32 kg. The pelage is dusky gray to pale yellow with large, dark squarish, oval and rosette marking. The belly and innersides of the limbs are pale.

Habits Inhabits various types of subtropical forests up to altitudes of 2000 – 2500 m. Are solitary, nocturnal and highly arboreal. They can pounce on ground prey such as rabbits and Reeve's muntjac from over-hanging branches.

Reproduction Birth occurs from March to August. The gestation period is 86 – 92 days, with 1 – 5 kittens, usually 2. Weaned at 5 months of age.

Distribution Qinlin Mts. region and southern China.

Conservation China: II; INCN: VU; CITES: appendix I.

Panthera pardus Leopard

Description Head and body 100 – 191 cm, tail 58 – 110 cm, and weight 37 – 90 kg for males, and 28 – 60kg for females. The body is grayish yellow with black spots that are grouped in rosettes.

Habits Inhabits and adapts to various kinds of forested environments. It is solitary and nocturnal. Feeds on small deer, wild pigs and rabbits.

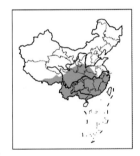

Reproduction Mating occurs in February. The estrous cycle is 46 days, gestation lasts 90 – 105 days after which the female gives birth to 2 – 3 cubs. There is one litter per year, which are weaned at 3 months of age. Reach sexual maturity at 2.5 – 3 years of age. Life span reach up to 20 – 23 years in captivity.

Distribution Northeast China and south of yellow River. Very rare.

Conservation China: I; CITES: appendix I.

Neofelis nebulosa

Panthera pardus

129

Panthra uncia Snow leopard

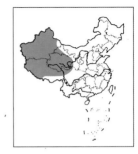

Description Head and body 110 – 130 cm, tail 80 – 90 cm, and weight 38 – 75 kg. The head is relatively small and round. The fur is dense and long. The length of fur on the back is 3 cm and on the underside is 6.5 cm. The body color is grayish yellow. On the back and sides there are large irregular black circles and rosettes.

Habits Inhabits high rocky mountain areas. In summer the animal lives above snow line or in alpine meadows at altitudes of 3000 – 4000 m. In winters it migrates with its prey down into coniferous forest at altitudes of 1500 – 2000 m. It is solitary and nocturnal, but most active at dust and dawn. Feeds on small ungulates, marmots, wild pigs, birds, rabbits and other animals.

Reproduction Mating occurs in late spring. The estrous cycle is 54 – 70 days, the gestation period is 90 – 103 days. The female gives birth to 2 – 3 cubs in June and July. The cubs attain sexual maturity at around 2 years. The life span is 15 years and 8 months in captivity.

Distribution Northwest China. Rare in number.

Conservation China: I; IUCN: EN; CITES: appendix I.

Panthra uncia

Head of a snow leopard

Panthera tigris `Tiger`

Description Head and body 140 – 280 cm, tail 60 – 90 cm. The tiger is the largest living cat. The siberian tiger, is the heaviest subspecies, males weigh 180 – 306 kg and females 90 – 120 kg. The South China tiger subspecies, males weigh 149.6 – 225 kg and females 90 – 120 kg. The front paws have long, sharp retractile claws. The ears are short and rounded, the back of the ears are black with is a white spot. The upper part of the body is reddish orange to red brown or orangish yellow. The body and legs have a series of narrow black transverse stripes, in some areas there are double stripes.

Habits Inhabits a wide variety of habitats. But primarily a forest dweller. It is mainly nocturnal and solitary except when in heat, mating and rearing the young. Feeds mainly on large mammals, especially ungulates, but also birds, reptiles, fish, frogs, crabs, locusts, and other animals. A tiger can prey on sambar or buffalo that weigh 160 – 400 kg, but usually preys on species that weigh 10 – 100 kg. The tiger can consume up to 17 – 27 kg at a time.

Reproduction Mating occurs mainly in January and February. The estrous cycle is 46 days, the estrous period is 6 – 7 days, and the gestation period is 90 – 105 day. The female gives birth every 1 – 2 years. Litter size 1 – 6 cubs, usually 2 – 3 cubs. The cubs at birth weigh 500 – 600 g, opens their eyes after 10 days and are weaned at 3 months. Before becoming independent the young stay with their mother for a period of 18 – 24 months. The tiger becomes sexually mature at about 3 years of age. The longevity in captivity is around 23 years.

Distribution Northeast China and south China. The numbers are less than 100.

Conservation China: I; IUCN: EN; CITES appendix I.

Panthera tigris corbetti

Panthera tigris altaica

Panthera tigris amoyensis

PINNIPEDIA

The pinnipeds are highly aquatic carnivores. Their bodies are streamlined and covered with a thick coat of short hair. The limbs are modified into flippers. The tail is short. They spend most of their life in the water, but return to land to bear their young. There are 3 families with 34 species in the world, of these only 2 families and 5 species are found in coastal waters of China. The larga seals have been known to breed in Bohai sea, the other 4 species are seen occasionally off Chinese waters. The 2 families are:

Otariidae
Phocidae

Otariidae

The main features of this family are that the forelimbs are longer then the hind limbs; the hind foot can be turned forward to support their body weight to move on land. They have external ears about 5 cm in length. There are 14 species in the world, of these 2 species enter Chinese waters.

Callorhinus ursinus
* *Eumetopias jubata*

Callorhinus ursinus Northern fur seal

Description Head and body about 250 cm, and weight 300 kg for males, and females 145 cm, and weight 60 kg. The limbs are developed into flippers. The 4 limbs enable the animal to move on land. The ears are almost hidden beneath the fur. The flippers have sparse hair and the innersides naked. The back is silver gray to reddish brown, and the under parts reddish brown, the sides pale yellow. Newborns are entirely black.

Habits Spends most of the year at sea and do not come ashore during the non-breeding period. Feeds mainly on fish and mollusks. Ever year the fur seals migrate and assemble in large numbers at their breeding grounds from May to July.

Reproduction Mating occurs in May and July. A single young is born each year after about 12 months of gestation. Usually after 6 days of birth the female ovulates and mates. The females have an interval nursing feeding cycle with their cub of 2 – 3 day. The cubs are weaned at 2 – 4 months of age. The young males reach sexual maturity at 5 years, and for females at 3 – 4 year. The peak pregnancy rate is when females reach 8 – 16 years of age. Life span is 15 – 22 years.

Distribution Yellow Sea.

Conservation China: II; IUCN: VU.

Callorhinus ursinus

Phocidae

The characteristics of this family are that the forelimbs are shorter than the hind limbs, the hind flippers are turned posteriorly, and cannot rotate forward, or under the trunk. The hind limbs are used for swimming but are not able to support their body weight. They have no external ears. There are 10 genera and 19 species in the world. Three species are found in China.

* *Phoca largha*
Phoca hispida
Erignathus barbatu

Phoca largha Larga seal

Description Head to body 150 – 200 cm. Males are larger than females. Males weigh about 150 kg, and females weigh 120 kg. The body is stocky yet streamlined, they have a broad head with large eyes, and a wide short snout. The flippers are furred. The tail is short. The adult pelage is grayish yellow or dark gray on the back with numerous spots. Underparts are creamy yellow. The pubs are covered with a dense, soft creamy white coat at birth.

Habits Inhabits high latitude temperate oceanic zones. This species is not gregarious, but during the breeding season, males and females live in pairs on ice floes and breed. After the pubs are born family groups are formed. When searching for food or resting, groups of up to 10 individuals gather in a area. Feeds on fish, squid, crustaceans.

Reproduction Mating occurs in March. This is the only pinniped that breeds in China, the most southernly latitude of its breeding areas. In the beginning of November the seals enter Liaodong bay of Bohai Sea in pairs. A single pub is born on the ice floes from January to February after a gestation of 11 months. Weaned at 1 month of age. The newborn pub is covered with creamy white fur.

Distribution Bohai Sea and Yellow Sea. Few individuals are found in the East China Sea on the coast of Fujian.

Conservation China: II.

Phoca largha

137

CETACEA

The cetaceans are strictly aquatic mammals highly adapted for life at sea or rivers. The body is streamlined and fishlike in appearance. Hair is virtually lacking on the body and there is a thick layer of blubber under the skin. The forelimbs are peddle – shaped and the hind limbs are absent. The tail is flattened and horizontal. There are 1 – 2 nasal openings at the top of the head. There are no external ears, and the eyes are very small. There are 2 mammae situated in grooves on each side of the genital opening. The male's testes are situated in the body cavity. Cetaceans are divided into suborder of Odontoceti and Mystacoceti. There are 10 families and about 75 species in the world. Most of the species are oceanic, but some inhabit fresh water. There are 8 families and 31 species in Chinese waters and rivers.

ODONTOCETI

The characteristics of odontoceti are that they all have teeth and only 1 blowhole. There is no caecum. Feeds on squid, fish and other large animals.

Platanistidae	1	species
Delphinidae	15	species
Phocoenidae	1	species
Physeteridae	3	species
Ziphiidae	3	species

MYSTACOCETI

Large sized cetaceans, characterized by 2 blowholes on the head and on each side of the upper jaw there are 150 – 400 of baleen plates instead of teeth. There is a caecum. Feeds on krills and other small crustaceans.

Eschrichtiidae	1	species
Balaenopteridae	6	species
Balaenidae	1	species

Odontoceti（teeth）

Mystacoceti（baleen plates）

CETACEA

Platanistidae

The beaklike snout is long and narrow, which accounts for about 15% of the head and body length. There are more than 120 teeth on the upper and lower jaws. Live in fresh water rivers and lakes. There are 4 genera and 4 species in the world, but only the white fin dolphin occurs in China.

Lipoteds vexillifer Baiji

Description Head to tail 1.5 – 2.5 m, and weight 100 – 200 kg, males may reach up to 237 kg. The beak is about 30 cm. The eyes are very small, situated above the corners of the mouth. The ears are tiny, found just behind the eyes. A single blowhole is located slightly left of center on the top of the head. The dorsal fin is triangular and the flippers are broad and rounded at the ends. The fluke are notched. There are 30 – 35 teeth on each side of the upper and lower jaws. The dolphins are pale grayish blue above and white below.

Habits Inhabits fresh water lakes and rivers. Mostly found in rich food environments especially in branches of rivers, sand bars, mouth of lakes. They are active at dawn and dust. Swims in pods of 2 – 7 individuals, sometimes single or in groups of more than 10 individuals. The dolphins rise to the surface to breathe every 10 – 20 seconds. Feeds on fish that weighs less than 1 kg.

Reproduction Mating occurs from April to May. A calf is born annually from March to August. The newborn weighs 5 kg at birth. Females reach sexual maturity when 6 years old (head and tail length 200 cm) and males at 4 year of age (head and tail length over 180 cm).

Distribution Endemic species of China. The species is restricted to mid and lower Yangzi River. Estimated population less than 100.

Conservation China: II; IUCN: CR; CITES: appendix I.

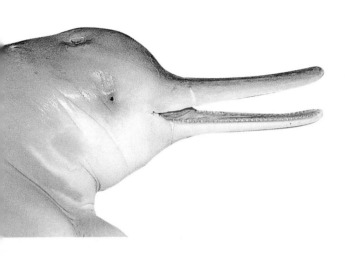

Lipoteds vexillifer

141

Delphinidae

They are small and medium representatives of order Cetacea. Head to tail length is less than 4 meters. The snouts are not long, the teeth are sharp and small. The tail fluke is notched in the middle. There are 34 species in the world, at least 15 species are found in Chinese waters. The species are as follows:

* *Steno bredanensis*
  Sousa chinensis
  Stenella attenuata
  Stenella coeruleoalba
  Stenella frontalis
  Stenella longirostris
* *Delphinus delphis*
  Delphinus tropicalis

Tursiops truncatus
lagenodelphis hosei
Lagenorhynchus obliquidens
Peponocephala electra
Pseudorca crassidens
* *Orcinus orca*
  Grampus griseus

Sousa chinensis
Chinese white dolphin

Description Head to tail 160 – 250 cm, and weight about 150 kg, to as heavy as 235 kg. The beak and forehead is separated by a V shaped groove. The body color is creamy white with distinctive gray spots on the back, the underpart is pink. In young individuals the back is grayish black and belly is white.

Habits Inhabits river estuaries and bays of tropical and subtropical waters. It lives in pods from a few individuals to as many as 20. Feeds mainly on fish.

Reproduction Mating occurs in June and July. The gestation period is 10 months. Birth takes place from March to April. The length of the newborn is 1/3 that of the females. Lactation lasts 3 – 4 months. Sexually mature in 2 – 3 years. Life span 25 – 35 years.

Distribution South Sea waters, seldom found along Zhejiang coastal waters and in the mouth of the Yangzi River.

Conservation China: I; CITES: appendix I.

Sousa chinensis

CETACEA

Delphinus delphis Common dolphin

Description Head and tail 150 – 250 cm, and weight 60 – 75 kg. The beak is long. The dorsal fin is triangular and the pectoral flippers have pointed ends. The back is bluish to blackish gray.

Habits Inhabits temperate and tropical waters. It has a habit of following fishing boats and steam boats. Swims in pods of 10 – 100 individuals, sometimes in large groups of up to several hundred. Feeds on fish and cephalopods.

Reproduction Mating occurs in January to April and August to September. The female gives birth in the second year from March to May and August to October. The gestation period is 10 – 11 months and lactation lasts 5 – 6 months. Annually I litter. Reach sexually mature in 3 – 5 years. The life span is about 20 – 25 years.

Distribution Coastal waters of China.

Conservation China: II; CITES: appendix II.

Orcinus orca Killer whale

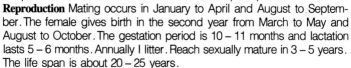

Description Head to tail in males 670 – 980 cm, weighs up to 9000 kg. Females smaller than males. Dorsal fin height is 180 cm. The pectoral flippers and tail fluke are broad adapted for rapid swimming. Very distinctive black and white patterning. The back and sides are black and the belly white.

Habits Inhabits of all oceans and seas, especially the Arctic and Anarctic. They live in groups of 2 – 40 individuals. Feeds mainly on fish, octopus and also on dolphins and pennipeds.

Reproduction Mating occurs throughout the year. The gestation lasts 13 – 16 months. One calving per year. Sexual maturity is reached in females at 4 years of age. Life span reaches 50 years in captivity.

Distribution Coastal waters of China. Frequently seen in the Yellow Sea and Bohai Sea.

Conservation China: II; CITES: appendix II.

Delphinus delphis

Orcinus orca

145

Ziphiidae

Medium sized cetaceans. There are V shaped grooves that converg anteriorly on the throat. Flippers are narrow and tail fluke wide. The dorsal fin is located near the tail fluke. There are 6 genera and 18 species in the world, of these 2 genera and 3 species are found in the waters of China.

Mesoplodon ginkgodens
* *Mesoplodon densirostris*

* *Ziphius cavirostris*

Ziphus cavirostris Goose-beaked whale

Description Head to tail 550 – 700 cm, and weight about 3000 kg. The beak is short and thick, the forehead is not pronounced. There are no teeth in the upper jaw and the low jaw has only 1 pair of functional teeth, the rest are vestigial teeth. The back is brownish gray and the ventral paler or pinkish.

Habits Inhabits all seas and oceans. Swims in groups of 3 – 5 individuals. Feeds on a wide variety of food. It is fond of squid, the diet also includes button fish, sea cucumbers, starfish, crabs and other marine animals.

Reproduction The gestation period is 1 year and gives birth in summer and autumn. Annually single calf. Life span over 20 years.

Distribution Taiwan waters

Conservation China: II; CITES: appendix II.

Mesoplodon densirostris
Blainville's beaked whale

Brief description Found in warm waters. Head and tail can reached 450 cm. The body is black, streamlined, flattened laterally, body height is greater than body width.

Distribution Coastal waters of Taiwan.

Conservation China: II; CITES: appendix II.

Ziphus cavirostris

CETACEA

Phocoenoidae

This family consists of small cetacean. Head and tail length is less than 2.5 meters. The upper jaw and the low jaw are about the same length, and lack a beak. It has no dorsal fin. There are 6 species in the world. China has only 1 species.

Neophocaena phocaenoidae
Finless porpoise

Description Head to tail 120 – 160 cm, and weight 25 – 50 kg, but can reach 220 kg. Stocky bodies. Head is round and has no beak. The flippers are large and slightly triangular. It has no dorsal fin, but has 3 – 4 cm wide skin fold humps on the back. The back is bluish gray, and paler or pale red below.

Habits Inhabits coastal waters and in bays of tropical and warm temperate areas. It lives in both salt and freshwater, but is frequently found at boundaries where salt water and fresh water mix. Usually seen singly, but sometimes in groups of 2 – 5 individuals. In breeding season it associates in groups of up to 20 individuals. When the animals are frightened they can stay submerged for 8 – 12 minutes. Feeds mainly on shrimps, fish and squid and especially on anchovy during the fishing season of the Yangzi River estuary.

Reproduction Mating occurs in Februarys to July. The gestation period is 11months. Births occur in April to August. Annually bear one litter with one young, seldom twins. Lactation lasts 5 – 12 months. Reach sexual maturity in 2 year.

Distribution Coastal waters and often enters upper and middle reaches of rivers.

Conservation China: II; CITES: appendix I.

Neophocaena phocaenoides

Physeteridae

The characteristics of this family are that they have enormous heads and blunt snouts, only the lower jaw has functional teeth. There are 2 genera and 3 species in the world and all are found in Chinese waters.

Kogia breviceps   * Physeter macrocephalus
Kogia simus

Physeter macrocephalas Sperm whale

Description Head to tail length averages 12.2 meters, but in males maximum length may reach 20 meters, and females 8.5 meters. They weight 35 000 – 50 000 kg. It is the largest species of teethed whales. The head is enormous. The pectoral fins are 2 meters long; no dorsal fin, and the width of the tail fluke is 4 – 4.5 meters. The entire body is bluish gray, but the underside is paler. Near the corners of the mouth the skin is grayish white.

Habits Inhabits tropical and subtropical waters. Swims in groups of 20 – 40 individuals. Feeds on large squid and fish.

Reproduction Mating takes place mainly in April. Births occur in autumn. Gestation period is 14 – 17 months. Annually 1 litter and 1 calf. When born the young are about 400 cm in length and weigh about 1000kg. Lactation lasts about 2 years. The females reach sexual maturity at 7 – 9 years, but they actually breeds at 25 – 27 years. Life span is up to 77 years.

Distribution Taiwan waters.

Conservation China: II; CITES: appendix I.

Physeter macrocephalus

Balaenopteridae

This family includes the largest whales. The head and tail length is 10 – 30 m. They have many longitudinal grooves on the throat and belly, and a small dorsal fin. There are more than 400 baleen plates on each side of the upper jaw. Occur throughout all the oceans and seas. There are 2 genera and 6 species all of these species are found in Chinese waters. The list is as follows:

Balaenoptera acutorostrata   Balaenoptera musculus
Balaenoptera edeni   * Balaenoptera physalus
Balaenoptera borealis   Megaptera novaeangliae

Balaenoptera acutorostrata Minke whale

Brief description In Chinese waters the head to tail length averages 693 cm, and weight 2200 kg, the largest may reach 4800 kg. Mainly found in Arctic, Anarctic to subtropical waters. Prefers continental sea and near coastal waters. Swims in small groups of 2 – 3 individuals. Feeds on small fish and krills. Mating takes place from September to October. Births occur in June and July. Annually 1 litter. Sexual maturity at 4 years of age.
Distribution Chinese waters.
Conservation China: II; CITES: appendix I.

Balaenoptera acutorostrata

Balaenoptera physalus Fin whale

Description Head to tail length at sexual maturity about 16 – 20m in males and 18.3 m for females. Maximum length is 25 m and weight 45 000 kg. The dorsal fin is small, about 61 cm high. There are 350 – 400 baleen plates on each side of the upper jaw and 50 – 60 throat grooves. The color is blackish brown above and white below.

Habits They are pelagic migratory species. In summer they move into cold temperate waters to feed and in winter they return to warm temperate waters to breed. They are deep divers and may dive to depths of 230 m and can stay submerged for 15 minutes. They live in small groups of 6 – 7 individuals but sometimes up to 50 individuals. Feeds mainly on krills and small crustaceans.

Reproduction Breeds every 2 – 3 years. The gestation period is 11.5 months. The newborn is about 650 cm in length and weigh 1800 kg. The lactation lasts 6 months. Sexual maturity at 6 – 8 years of age. Some individuals live up to 114 years.

Distribution Entersouth China Sea, East China Sea and Yellow Sea to breed and to forage.

Conservation China: II; IUCN: EN; CITES: appendix I.

Balaenoptera physalus

CETACEA

Eschrichtiidae

There is only a single species in the world and it also occurs in Chinese waters.

Eschrichtius robustus Gray whale

Description Head to tail 13 – 17 m, and weight 20 000 – 37 000 kg. There are 140 – 180 baleen plates on the upper jaw. The bluish gray back has no dorsal fin.

Habits Inhabits shallow waters of Pacific Ocean and Arctic coasts. Swims alone or in small groups. Feeds mainly on plankton, crustaceans and small fish.

Reproduction Mating occurs in early winter. Breeds every 2 years and has a gestation period of 13 months, the calf attains sexual maturity at 8 years.

Distribution Yellow Sea to Guangzhou Bay and Hainan Island waters of South China Sea.

Conservation China: II; CITES: appendix I.

Balaenidae

There are no longitudinal grooves on the throat. There are 2 genera and 3 species in the world and only 1 species is found in Chinese waters.

Balaema glacialis Black right whale

Description Head to tail 13.6 – 16.6 meters, and weight 20000 – 67000kg. There is no dorsal fin, the pectoral flippers are large and broad. On each side of the upper jaw are 250 baleen plates. Color grayish blue in young individuals and bluish black or black in adults.

Habits Inhabits in all oceans. Active on the water surface. It swims slowly. Feeds exclusively on small crustaceans.

Reproduction Mating occurs in the winter. The gestation period is 12 months. A single calf is born every 2 – 3 years.

Distribution During reproduction and foraging the migration enters the Yellow Sea, East China Sea and eastern South China Sea waters.

Conservation China: II; IUCN: EN; CITES: appendix I.

Eschrichtius robustus

Balaema glacialis

SIRENIA

The sirenias are large mammals and completely aquatic. The skin is thick with many skin folds, and practically hairless on the surface except for the stiff vibrissae around the lips. The eyes are small, lack of external ears, and the neck is short. The forelimbs are modified into paddles, the hind limbs are absent. Occurs in shallow seas and river mouths. There are 4 living species under 2 family, and 2 genera in the world. Of these only 1 family (Dogongidae) 1 genus and 1 species occurs in China.

Dugong dugon Dugong

DescriptionThirteen specimens from Baibu Bay, Guangxi yielded the following data: In males the head to tail length 237.3 (205-257) cm, and body weight 240 (200-285) kg. Females head to tail length 281 (260-318) cm, and weight 386 (320-481) kg, The largest may reach a weight of 650 kg. The head is small, and the skin is thick about 1 – 1.5 cm. The tail is flattened horizontally, notched and crescent shaped. The body is covered with hard scattered hair. The color of adults dull brown and young are pale brown.

Habits Inhabits shallow coastal waters in tropical regions where vegetation is abundant. The dugong is herbivorous. Feeds on salty plants and large leafed seaweeds The dugongs are active at day in social groups of 4 – 5 individuals, sometimes numbering more than 10 individuals. The old individuals live singly. The dugong rises above the surface every 2 – 6 minutes and breathe for 2 seconds, the longest dive period is 16 – 25 minutes.

Reproduction Breeds throughout the year. The gestation period is 11 – 13 months and 1 young per litter. The young begin feeding in 3 months. Life span is estimated to be 40 years.

Distribution Shallow coastal waters of Taiwan, Guangdong and Guangxi.
Conservation China: I; IUCN: VU; CITES: appendix I.

Dugong dugon

The Dugong swims in shallow water

PROBOSCIDEA

They are the largest living land mammals, weighing 5000 – 7500 kg. Elephants are characterized by their immense size and sensitive agile, long trunk. The shoulder height is 3 – 4 meters, the legs are bulky and strong. The skin is thick and only a few stiff hairs on the body. In adult males the upper incisors form tusks. There is 1 family (Elephantidae) with 2 genera and 2 species in the world of these only 1 species is distributed in China.

Elaphas maximus Asiatic elephant

Description Head and body (Including the trunk) 550 – 640 cm, tail 120 – 150 cm, shoulder height 250 – 300 cm, and weight about 5000 kg. The skin color is gray to tang. The males have tusks, which reach a length of 1.5 – 1.8 meters. The tusks of females are short and cannot see outside. In contrast with the African elephants, the ears are relatively small and at the tip of the trunk has only one fingerlike process.

Habits Inhabits tropical environments from dense forests to grasslands. Active in the morning and in the evening. Females are gregarious and males mostly live alone. Feeds on a variety of grasses, bark, twigs and thin branches, it also takes banana, paddy and sugar cane.

Reproduction Breeding occurs all year. The estrous cycle for females averages 22 days and the estrus is 4 days. The average gestation period is 646 (615 – 668) days. A single young are is born, which weighs 107 (50 – 150) kg at birth. The young are covered with light brown hair which it will gradually lose as they grow. Females reach sexual maturity at 9 – 12 years of age, and males at about 10 – 17 years of ages. The life span is 69 years.

Distribution Southern Yunnan. Very rare.

Conservation China: I; IUCN: EN; CITES; appendix I.

Asiatic elephants in a group

Elaphas maximus (♂)

PERISSODACTYLA

These are large hoofed animals. Some species are modified for fast running (such as the equidae), and some species are heavily built animals (such as the rhinocerotidae). The major characteristic is that only the third digit of the hind feet is well developed and functional. There are 3 families and 5 species in the world, of these 1 family with 2 species live in China.

Equidae
Equus przewalskii
Equus hemionus

Equus przewalskii Wild horse

Description Head and body 220 – 280 cm, shoulder height 120 – 146 cm, and weight 200 – 300 kg, can reach up to 350 kg. The neck has a short, stiff, and erect mane, which extends from the head to the shoulders. The tail is long with long hair at the base and tip. They do not have a long forelock as does the domestic horses.

Habits Inhabits deserts, steppes, hilly lands, gobi and areas of grassland. The wild horse gathers in family groups organized into harems of 6 – 15 individuals. The harem includes a dominant stallion, several mares and their young. The animals move freely in the wild. Feeds on various kinds of desert plant matter. In winter eats withered grass and moss.

Reproduction Mating occurs in June. Gestation lasts 320 – 340 days, a single foal is born in April to May. Sexual maturity at 2.5 years. Life span is about 30 years, the highest record was 34 years.

Distribution Zhun Ge'er Basin of Xinjiang. Extinct in its natural habitat.

Conservation China: I; CITES: appendix I. Reintroduce into its original habitat, under semi-captivity.

Equus przewalskii

Wild horse in a group

Equus hemionus Asiatic wild ass

Description Head and body 189 – 214 cm, tail 31 – 45 cm, shoulder height 126 – 128 cm, and weight 200 – 270 g. The coat color is brown or dark brown. The mane is dark brown, short and erect. There is a narrow dark blackish brown stripe on the back extending from the shoulders to the base of the tail. The innersides of the thighs and belly are white or grayish white.

Habits Inhabits drought deserts, semi-drought deserts, steppes and mountain deserts at altitudes of 200 – 5100 m. Feeds on desert plants and halophytes. Active by day. At night they rest among low bushes. The wild ass lives in small groups of 5 – 15 individuals, occasionally gathers in large groups of 200 – 300 individuals.

Reproduction Mating occurs from August to September. The females breed every 2 years. Gestation lasts 11 months, birth takes place from June to July and a single foal is born. The females reach sexual maturity at 3 year of age and males 4 years of age. Life span in captivity is 14 years.

Distribution Qingzang plateau and northwest desert areas. Numbers estimated to be over 10 000 individuals.

Conservation China: I; IUCN: VU; CITES: appendix II.

A group of Asiatic wild ass

Equus hemionus hemionus

Equus hemionus kiang

ARTIODACTYLA

The feature of even-toed ungulates is that the third and fourth toes are well developed to support the body weight. The first toe has been lost in evolution and second and fifth toes are vestigial. Most species developed horns or antlers, in a few species the canines are enlarged and elongated like tusks. All even – toed ungulates are ruminants and have a three chambered or four chambered stomach, except for the suidae. Feeds on plants. There are 10 families and 194 living species in the world. Of these 6 families and 44 species are found in China. The 6 families are as follows:

Suidae	1	species
Camelidae	1	species
Tragulidae	1	species
Moschidae	5	species
Cervidae	16	species
Bovidae	20	species

Suidae

The feature of this family is that they have short legs, the body is covered with coarse bristly hairs with no under fur. The snout is elongated and has a mobile, agile disklike tip. The nostrils opens at the terminal. They are omnivorous and have only one chambered stomach thus are not ruminants. There are 5 genera and 8 species in the world, but only 1 species is native to China.

Sus scrofa Wild boar

Description Head and body 90 – 180 cm, tail 20 – 30 cm, and weight 50 – 200 kg. The snout is longer than the domesticated pigs. The ears are erect. In males the upper canines form well developed tusks and protrude outward from the lips to a length of 7 – 13 cm.

Habits Inhabits in a wide variety of habitats, but prefer dense shrublands, humid broad leafed forests or grasslands. They are active all day, especially in the morning and in the evening. They are gregarious animals and live in family groups headed by a female pig. Feeds on omnivorous diets includes green vegetation, roots, bulbs, tubers, fruits and also small vertebrates and invertebrates.

Reproduction Mating occurs in winter. The young are born in the spring. The estrus cycle is 21 days, the gestation period is 114 – 140 days. One litter annually with 4 – 8 young. Lactation lasts 2 – 3 months. They reach sexual maturity in 8 – 10 months of age, but the females usually mate at 1.5 years of age. The life span is 20 – 25 years in captivity.

Distribution Southern and northern parts of China.

Sus scrofa

ARTIODACTYLA

Camelidae

This family has two important characteristics; the foot has only 2 toes and it has a 3 chambered stomach. There are 3 genera and 4 species in the world, of these only the Bactrian camel inhabits China.

Camelus ferus Bactrian camel

Description Head and body 320 – 350 cm, and weight 450 – 650 kg. The neck is long and slender, the ears are small and haired. It has a slitlike nostril that can close to keep out dust and sand. The feet have only the third and fourth toes and the rest of the toes are only vestigial. The animal have 2 humps.

Habits Inhabits the Gobi plains. The animals can withstand heat, cold, thirst and coarse fodder. They live alone or in groups. In the winter may gather in groups of 30 individuals. Feeds on vegetation that grows in the Gobi desert. In the autumn fat is stored in the erect humps, which is used in the severe winter for food.

Reproduction Mating occurs in spring. The gestation period is 390 – 410 days. Gives birth in summer in the second year. They breed every other year. Litters contain a single calf. At 4 years of age the young reach sexual maturity. The life span is up to 30 – 50 years.

Distribution Northwest China, mainly occurs in Xinjiang.

Conservation China: I; IUCN: EN.

Camelus ferus

ARTIODACTYLA

Tragulidae

These are the smallest species of ungulates and weigh 1.2 – 13 kg. They resembles the muntjacs, but do not have antlers. The stomach is 3 chambered and are ruminants. There are 3 genera with 3 species only the Lesser Malay chevrotain is found in China.

Tragulus javanicus
Lesser Malay chevrotain

Description Head and body 42 – 48 cm, tail 5 – 8 cm, and weight 1.2 – 2.5 kg. The pelage is brown with white or pale yellow spots or stripes on the back and sides. The underparts are white. There are no antlers, but the male has well developed tusks.

Habits Inhabits tropical lowland forests and shrublands. They are nocturnal and solitary in habit. Feeds on tender leaves of low shrubs, fallen fruits or berries.

Reproduction Two litters per year. The gestation period is 140 – 170 days. There is usually 1 young, occasionally 2. The females have a post-partum oestrus within 2 day after giving birth and are ready to mate. Sexual maturity is in 5 months. Life span is 14 years in captivity.

Distribution Southern Yunnan.

Conservation China: I.

Head of the lesser Malay chevrotain showing the tusk

Tragulus javanicus

ARTIODACTYLA

Moschidae

The moschidae are small artiodactyla, weigh only 6 – 15 kg. Neither sex processes antlers, but the upper canines of the males are well developed into tusks. It is sharp and about 5 – 6 cm long. They have a gall bladder. Lack a facial gland, frontal gland and suborbital gland, but have a well developed caudal gland under the tail. The males have a musk sac situated between the umbilicus and penis which produces musk, a oily secretion that is highly valued. Due to the economic value of musk, the animal is being driven toward extinction. There is 1 genus with 5 species, all are distributed in China.

* *Moschus moschiferus*
* *Moschus berezovskii*
* *Moschus fuscus*
* *Moschus chrysogaser* = (*M. Sifanieus*)
* *Moschus leucogaster*

Moschus moschiferus
Siberian musk deer

Description Head and body 65 – 85 cm, tail 4 – 6 cm, and weight 8 – 12 kg. The tail is short and not shown. There are 4 – 5 longitudinal rows of cinnamon color spots on the body. The neck stripes are white.

Habits Inhabits mountain needle forests or mixed needle and broad leafed forests. They are solitary and are active at dawn and dust. They have a wide variety of food. Feeds chiefly on tender leaves of shrubs, herds and lichens.

Reproduction Mating occurs in winter. The estrous cycle is 19 – 25 days, the gestation period is a about 6 months, and birth takes place from May to June. There are 1 – 3 young, mostly 2 in a litter. Lactation lasts 3 months and they become sexual maturity at about 1.5 years. The life span is 17 years in captivity.

Distribution Forested areas of north Xinjiang, northeast China and Dabei Mts. Estimated less than 10 000 head.

Conservation China: II; IUCN: VU; CITES: appendix II.

Moschus fuscus Black musk deer

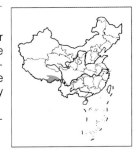

Brief description Weight about 8 kg. Color black, in some individuals the shoulders are brownish yellow. Neck has white stripes. Inhabits forest edges of high mountain needle leafed forests and in areas of high rocky mountains.

Distribution Northwest of Yunnan and eastern fringes of Xizang. Very rare.

Conservation China: II; CITES: appendix II.

Moschus leucogaster

Himalayan musk deer

Brief description Weight 11 – 15 kg. The back is dull brown, the rump is yellowish white. No neck stripes. Inhabits mixed forest of high mountain and alpine steppes. Feeds on various shrubs and weeds.

Distribution Fringe of southern Himalayan slops, rare.

Conservation China: II CITES: appendix II.

Moschus moschiferus

169

ARTIODACTYLA

Moschus berezovskii Forest musk deer

Description Head and body 70 – 80 cm, tail about 4 cm, and weight 6 – 9 kg. There are no spots on the back and sides in adults, but has distinctive white or pale brown neck stripes.

Habits Inhabits needle leafed, broad leafed forest or mixed forest at altitudes of 2000 – 3800 m. They are solitary and are active in the morning and evening. They have the ability to jump easily along rugged terrain and climb steep slopes and cliffs. They can also jump in trees to eat leaves. Feeds mainly on tender leaves of woody plants and seldom eat grass.

Reproduction Mating peak occurs from November to December. The estrous cycle is 15 – 25 days, the gestation period is 176 – 183 days and births take place mainly in June. There are 1 – 3 young per litter, usually 2. The newborn weigh 0.5 kg at birth, and are marked with pale spots, which disappear at age of 2 months. The young are weaned at 3 month and become sexually mature in 1.5 years. Under captive conditions they can live more than 13 years.

Distribution Mainly distributed in southwest China, especially in Xizang and Sichuan. It is estimated that there are 100 000 individuals in the wild.

Conservation China: II; CITES: appendixn II.

Fawn of the forest musk deer

Moschus berezovskii

Forest musk deer feeding teeder leaves on a branch

Moschus chrysogaster Alpine musk deer

Description Head and body 85 – 90 cm, tail 6 – 7 cm, and weight 9.6 – 13 kg. In contrast with the forest musk deer the ears are much larger, the coat is sandy brown in color, and the neck has distinctive stripes. The tips of the ears are pale brownish yellow. The upper canines are well developed into tusks in the males, about 7 – 10 cm in length.

Habits Inhabits areas of alpine meadows, bare rocky mountains, fir forests, and shrublands up to 2000 – 4000 m. They are solitary and active at dust and dawn. During the estrous period, they are gregarious, living in small groups of 3 – 7 individuals. Feeds mainly on leaves of shrubs and grass. In winter it takes lichens, pteridophyta, withered grass and fallen leaves.

Reproduction Mating occurs from November to January. The gestation period is 185 – 195 days and births take place mainly in June. There are 1 – 2 young per litter, usually 2. The young reach sexual maturity at 16 – 17 months of age.

Distribution Plateau areas of northwest China. It is estimated that there are about 100 000 individuals in the wild.

Conservation China: II; CITES: appendix II.

Fawn of an Alpine musk deer

Moschus chrysogaster

Shows the distintive stripes on the neckback

ARTIODACTYLA

Cervidae

This family has a wide range in body size, ranging from the smallest size muntjac weighing about 10 kg to the largest size moose, which exceeds 400kg. The male deer usually grows antlers, except for water deer in which both sexes lack antlers and in reindeer where both sexes grow antlers. The cervidae are characterized by; the bony core antlers that are forked and shed annually at a certain time; most of the species have a facial gland in front of the eye; they have no gall bladder. There are 13 genera and 38 species in the world. Of these there are 8 genera 16 species found in China.

- * *Hydropotes inermis*
- * *Elaphodus cephalophus*
- * *Muntiacus crinifrons*
- * *Muntiacus feae*
- * *Muntiacus muntjak*
- * *Muntiacus reevesi*
- * *Axis porcinus*
- * *Cervus albirostria*
- * *Cervus elaphus*

- * *Cervus eldi*
- * *Cervus nippon*
- * *Cervus unicolor*
- * *Elaphurus davidianus*
- * *Alces alces*
- * *Capreolus capreolus*
- * *Rangifer tarandus*
  （Semi-domesticated species）

Hydropotes inermis Chinese water deer

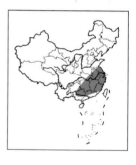

Description Head and body 91 – 103 cm, tail 6 – 7 cm, shoulder height 50 – 57 cm, and weight 14 – 17 kg. Neither sex has antlers. In males the upper canines are well developed into tusks and protrude outward below the upper jaw. The suborbital glands are very small and barely noticeable. The ears are large, the tail is tiny. The coat is yellowish brown in color. Fawns under 2 months of age have pale spotted coats.

Habits Inhabits among reeds, bushes and beard grass in swampy areas along rivers, lakes and coastal banks. They are also found on hillsides, and islands. They are solitary, active in the morning and evening. Feeds on tender leaves and buds of shrubs, but also takes grasses and other plant matter.

Reproduction Mating occurs in November and January. The gestation period is 6 – 7 months, the female gives birth from May to June. Litter size 2 – 5 offspring, but usually 2 – 3. Weaned after 3 months and become sexually mature by the end of the year.

Distribution Eastern parts of China in areas along rivers, lakes and coasts. It is estimated that there are about 10 000 individuals in the wild.

Conservation China: II.

Hydropotes inermis

Young Chinese water deer

Elaphodus cephalophus Tufted deer

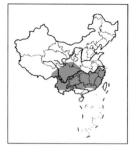

Description Head and body 82 – 119 cm, tail 8 – 13 cm, and weight 15 – 28 kg. There is no frontal gland (different from muntjac), but have a conspicuous pair of sub-orbital glands. The edge of the ears are white. There are long black hairs forming a horse shaped pattern on the forehead. Males have small antlers that do not furcate. The tail color is black dorsally and white ventrally.

Habits Inhabits subtropical mixed every green broad leafed and needle leafed forests. They live in pairs, active both in the morning and evening Feeds on forbs and tender leaves of shrubs, it also takes fungi and fallen fruits.

Reproduction Mating occurs in late autumn and early winter. The female gives birth in late spring and early summer. The gestation period is about 6 months. One young per litter. The females become sexually mature at the end of the year, but the males at 1.5 years of age. The life span is about 9 years.

Distribution Qinglin Mts. region and south of the Yangzi River. It is estimated that there are about 300 – 500 thousand surviving in the wild.

Muntiacus muntjak Indian muntjac

Description Head and body 100 – 135 cm, tail 16 – 20 cm, weight 22 – 30 kg. Both frontal glands and suborbital glands are well developed. The males have a pair of antlers with a single brow tine. The coat is deep brown to redish brown.

Habits Inhabits mountain forests. Live solitarily, but sometimes 2 – 4 individuals in a group. Feeds on tender leaves, buds, flowers of woody plants.

Reproduction Mates throughout the year. The gestation period is about 210 days, and gives birth to 1 young. The females have a post – partum oestrus, within 3 – 4 days after giving birth. Become sexually mature in 8 – 12 months. The life span is up to 10 years.

Distribution Forested areas of south China. It is estimated there are 150 – 300 thousand individuals surviving in the wild.

Elaphodus cephalophus

Muntiacus muntjak

177

Muntiacus crinifrons `Black muntjac`

Description Head and body 98 – 113 cm, tail 18 – 24 cm, and weight 21 – 28. 5 kg. It is similar to the Indian muntjac, but the body color is black brown. The head is brown and the distinguishing tuft on the forehead is yellowish brown. The back of the long tail is black and beneath white. The antlers are small with one tine.

Habits Inhabits broad leafed forests of sub-tropical mountains at elevations above 1000 m. They are active in the morning and evening. Feeds mainly on tender leaves of shrubs, but also takes weeds, ferns, fungi and fallen fruit.

Reproduction There is no specific breeding season. Lactation and pregnant females are found in all seasons. The gestation period is 6 – 7 months and they produce 1 fawn. Lactation lasts about 2 months. During lactation some females will conceive, but most females mate and conceive after lactation. The fawns are spotted with a pale color, which disappears when they are weaned. The females reach sexual maturity at 8 months of age. Under natural conditions the animals live for 10 – 11 years.

Distribution Western Zhejiang, southern Anhui and nearby provinces. It is estimated there are about 10 thousand individuals.

Conservation China: I; IUCN: VU; CITES: appendix I.

Muntiacus crinifrons

Head of a black muntjac

179

Muntiacus reevesi Chinese muntjac

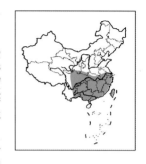

Description Head and body 70 – 96 cm, tail 9 – 15.5 cm, shoulder height 42 – 52 cm, and weight 10 – 15.2 kg. Adult males have small antlers with only 1 tine. The body is chestnut color. There are 2 black stripes running up from the innersides of the pedicles to the forehead. The tail black above and white below.

Habits Inhabits low mountains of subtropical forests, hilllands, secondary forests or shrublands. Lives along, or doe with a young family group can be seen together. Feeds in the morning and evening, on tender leaves, fruits, seeds of various vegetation, and fungi.

Reproduction Mating occurs throughout the year. Females produce 1 young, the gestation period is 6 – 7 months. Unlike other species of deer, the females have a post – partum estrous, reach early sexual maturity and usually conceive at 5 – 6 months of age. The fawn weighs about 1 kg at birth and is able to stand and walk after a few hours. The fawn is spotted with pale yellow which disappears when once weaned. Under natural conditions they may live for 8 years. In captivity the life span is over 13 years.

Distribution Southern Gansu, south of Qinlin Mts. range. There are about 2 000 000 – 2 500 000 in the wild.

Muntiacus reevesi (♂)

Muntiacus reevesi (♀)

181

Muntiacus feae Fea's muntjac

Description A small cervid. The body size and morphological features are similar to the Black muntjac. The head and body length is about 104 cm in adult males, tail about 15 cm, and shoulder height about 68 cm. The forehead and the pedicles are bright brown. They are different from the black muntjac in that they lack a long coronal tuft. The neck, back and sides are dull brown, the limbs nearly black. The inner thighs and groins are white. Tail back is black and below white.

Habits Inhabits mixed broad leaved and needle leaved forests and bunchshrub of plateau areas at altitudes below 2500 m They are solitary. Feeds on tender leaves of shrubs.

Distribution Eastern Xizang and Gaoligun Mts. of northwest Yunnan, very rare.

Axis porcinus Hog deer

Description Head and body 105 – 115 cm, tail about 20 cm, shoulder height 60 – 75 cm, and weight 36 – 50 kg. The antlers are long and slender with 3 tines. The summer coat is brownish yellow, the winter coat is pale brown or pale yellow.

Habits Inhabits forests. Lives single, but a few individuals may be together where food is abundant or during rut. Feeds on grasses, but also eats tender twigs, buds of trees and fallen fruit.

Reproduction Mating occurs throughout the year, but mainly in September and October. The gestation period is about 7 month, females produce 1 fawn, occasionally 2. The life span is 12 – 15 years, the maximum being 20 years.

Distribution Boundaries of Yunnan and Mynanmar. Rare in number.

Conservation China: I; CITES: appendix I.

Muntiacus feae

Axis porcinus

ARTIODACTYLA

Cervus unicolor Sambar

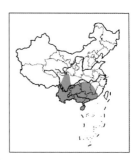

Description Head and body 170 – 200 cm, tail 22 – 30 cm, shoulder height 120 – 150 cm, and weight 100 – 250 kg. The body is stockily built. Males have a long bushy mane on the neck. The antlers have 3 tines each and the surface is coarse. The tail is long with long, loose, black bushy hair, which gives an appearance of a broad tail. The body color is dark brown, but in some individuals nearly black.

Habits Inhabits humid tropical and subtropical evergreen broad leaved forests, mixed needle and broad leaved forests, open grasslands and edge of woodlands. They are gregarious, usually a few individuals or up to more than a dozen in a herb. Active at night near water areas. In summer season, the males are fond of wallowing in quagmire areas or paddy fields. Feeds on grass, tree leaves, tender leaves, bamboo twigs and bamboo shoots.

Reproduction Mating occurs in autumn. The female gives birth during April and May, but in Hainan they breed throughout the year, and fawns are born in all seasons. The gestation period is 246 (211 – 295) days, usually birthing once a year or twice every 3 years. Lactation lasts about 6 months. Females reach sexual maturity at 1.5 – 2 years of age, males 2.5 – 3 years. Under natural conditions the animals may live for 11 – 12 years and in captivity the life span is about 20 years, the longest lived for 25 years.

Distribution Sichuan and south of Yangzi River. There are about 20 000 – 30 000 head in the wild.

Conservation China: II.

Cervus unicolor（♀）

Cervus unicolor（♂）

185

Cervus eldi *Thamin*

Description Head and body about 170 cm, tail about 25 cm, shoulder height 90 – 105 cm, and weight 70 – 100 kg in males, and females 60 kg. The body is yellowish brown, and there is a blackish brown stripe running along the back. In summer there are white spots on the sides. The brow tines point forward and curve upward, the beam facing backward and curves upward.

Habits Inhabits low hilllands or open grasslands of western Hainan. Usually 3 – 5 individuals in a herb, but during the mating season several dozen may assemble. Most active during the day. Feeds on various grasses, tender leaves of shrubs and tree leaves.

Reproduction Mating occurs from February to May. The gestation period is about 240 days, births occur from November to December. The female gives birth to a single fawn.

Distribution Western Hainan. The population recovered to 500 individuals in 1996.

Conservation China: I; IUCN: VU; CITES: appendix I.

Group of females

Cervus eldi (♂)

Cervus nippon Sika deer

Description Head and body 105 – 170 cm, tail 13 – 18 cm, shoulder height 85 – 110 cm, and weight 40 – 150 kg. The coats of adults and young are brown in summer with scattered white spots. The antlers usually have 4 tines.

Habits Inhabits broad leaved or mixed broad leaved and needle leaved forests, forest edges and grassplots at elevations of

300 – 3000 m. The Sika deer are gregarious, usually 5 – 6 individuals in a herb but sometimes up to 20 individuals.

Reproduction Mating occurs from September to October. The receptive period is 1 – 2 days, the gestation period lasts for 223 days and the females give birth to a single young in April and May. Lactation lasts about 4 months. The females are sexual maturity at 16 months of age, the males at 18 months. The life span is 25 years in captivity.

Distribution Distributed along the borders of Jiangxi, Anhui and Zhejiang with a population of about 200 individuals. In north Sichuan there is a population of 500. The wild population in Taiwan is extinct. As for the northeast China population some still may exist in the wild.

Conservation China: I.

Fawn with mother (Taiwan)

Cervus nippon (♂) (Sichuan)

Cervus nippon (♀)

Cervus elaphus Red deer

Description Head and body 165 – 265 m, tail 10 – 22 cm, shoulder 75 – 150 cm, and weight 75 – 200 kg. In male the brow antler beam extends from the pedicle and usually there are 5 – 6 tines. The body color is grayish brown with yellow or white spots on the rump.

Habits Inhabits a wide variety of habitats from level ground to alpine steppes, shrublands and edges of fir forests of high mountains exceeding 5000 m. They are active mainly in the morning and evening. Females cows and calves form small herds of 3 – 5 individuals, sometimes more than 10. Males usually are alone or in small groups. Feeds chiefly on grasses, tender leaves or green parts of shrubs.

Reproduction Mating occurs from September to November. The gestation period is about 235 days, females give birth to a single fawn in May and June. Lactation lasts for 9 months, become sexual maturity at 1.5 – 2.5 years of age. Under natural conditions the life span is about 14 years, but in captivity the maximum age is 26 years and 8 months.

Distribution Northeast and midwest China. There are about 100 000 in the wild.

Conservation China: II.

Cervus elaphus

Mother with fawn

A Tianshan stag

Cervus albirostris White lipped deer

Description Head and body about 210 cm, tail 10 – 13 cm, shoulder height about 130 cm, and weight about 250 kg. The coat is long, thick and coarse, generally yellowish brown or dull brown. The lips, chin and throat are white. There are 5 – 6 tines on each antler, and may be up to 8 or 9 tines.

Habits Inhabits high mountain alpine meadows and shrublands at altitudes of 3500 – 5000 m. At day they hide in the forest and gather in small herds of 4 – 5 individuals, sometimes up to a dozen. During the rutting season several dozen to more than 100 individuals may assemble. Feeds on grass and sedges, also takes other plant matter including tree bark.

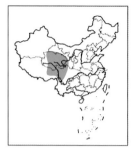

Reproduction Mating occurs in October. The gestation period is about 8 months. Gives birth to a single spotted young from May to June. The young become sexual maturity in the third year of life.

Distribution Native to China, only found in Sichuan and Qingzang plateau.

Conservation China: I; IUCN: VU.

Cervus albirostris

A pair of White lipped deer

Fawn and mother

ARTIODACTYLA

Elaphurus davidianus `Milu`

Description Head and body about 150 cm, tail about 50 cm, shoulder height about 115 cm, and weight 150 – 200 kg. The long tail ends with a tuft. The antlers have a distinctive structure in that the main bean extends upward and is not forked. The winter coat is grayish brown and the summer coat reddish brown.

Habits Inhabits marshlands and reed swamps of the plain areas. They are gregarious. Feeds on grass and aquatic plants.

Reproduction Mating occurs from June to August. The gestation period lasts for 250 – 170 days. Females give birth to 1 calf, sometimes 2 from April to May. Sexual maturity at 2 years and 3 months. The life span is about 20 years.

Distribution The past distribution of the Milu deer population is extinct in the coastal plain areas of eastern China. The semi-captive populations in Beijing and in Dafeng Reserve have increased from 38 in 1985 – 1987 to several hundred in the 90s. In 1994 the species were reintroduced onto a grassy island of 1.534 hectares in Shishou city of Hubei. There were about 107 free rangeing individuals in 1996.

Conservation China: I; IUCN: CR.

A bachelor group

A herb of both sexes

Elaphurus davidianus

Alces alces Moose

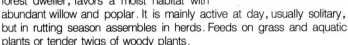

Description Head and body 200 – 260 cm, tail only about 10 cm, and weight 200 – 400 kg in males. The coat is brownish black to black. The head is large and long with a pendulous snout. The upper lip is long and broad. They have high humped shoulders. The males have massive palmate antlers.

Habits Inhabits cold needle forests. It is a forest dweller, favors a moist habitat with abundant willow and poplar. It is mainly active at day, usually solitary, but in rutting season assembles in herds. Feeds on grass and aquatic plants or tender twigs of woody plants.

Reproduction Mating occurs from September to October. A single calf, occasionally 2 are born in the late spring to early summer after a 240 – 250 days of gestation. The young are sexual maturity in 2 years. The life span in captivity is known to be 27 years.

Distribution About several thousand individuals in Da Xinggan Mts. and Xiao Xinggan Mts. In Altai Mts. has a low population.

Conservation China: II.

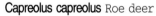

Capreolus capreolus Roe deer

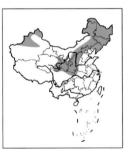

Description Head and body 95 – 140 cm, tail 2 – 4 cm, shoulder height 65 – 95 cm and weight 30 – 40 kg. Females are slightly smaller than males. The antlers has 3 tines and the main bean has knots. The coat is brown to yellowish brown. Fawns have a row of white spots on their sides.

Habits Inhabits slops of sparsely forested mountains, open shrublands and grass-lands. They are active both in the morning and evening, live alone or in small groups. Feeds on twigs of shrubs, various kinds of grasses, withered grass and lichens.

Reproduction Mating occurs in August and September. The gestation period is about 294 days (Including 4 – 5 months of delayed implantation). The birth of 2 fawns mainly occurs in June. Reach sexual maturity at 13 months of age. The life span is 10 – 12 years and the maximum is 17 years in captivity.

Distribution Northeast, north China and north Xinjiang.

Alces alces

Capreolus capreolus

Rangifer tarandus Reindeer

Description Head and body 120 – 220 cm. tail 7 – 21 cm shoulder height 94 – 127cm, and weight 91 – 272kg. Coloration varies widely, but generally brown or gray. Both sexes have antlers.

Habits Inhabits sub-cold coniferous forests. Most active by day. In Heilongjiang the semi-domesticated animals do not migrate and stay in Da Xinggan Lin Mts. throughout the year.

Reproduction Mating occurs mainly in October. Births take place in late May and early June. The gestation period is 227 – 229 days. The females give birth to 1 calf, rarely 2. The young are not spotted. Sexual maturity at 2.5 – 3.5 years.

Distribution The semi-domesticated reindeer of northeast China were originally introduced from north of Lake Baikal. There are now 800 – 900 individuals.

Rangifer tarandus

Bovidae

In the members of this family only the third and forth toes are well developed. The second and fifth toes are vestigial or absent. They are ruminants and have a four – chambered stomach. They have a gall bladder. In contrast with Cervidae, most members have a pair of unbranched true horns, which are present in both sexes and are never shed. The horn consists of a bony core outgrowth of the frontal bone and is covered by a sheath of dense keratinized epidermis. Both bony core and sheath grow continuously throughout life. There are 46 genera and 127 species in the world, of these 12 genera and 20 species are found in China.

* *Bos gaurus*
  Bos javanicus
* *Bos grunniens*
* *Gazella subgutturosa*
* *Procapra gutturosa*
* *Procapra picticaudata*
* *Procapra przewalskii*
* *Pantholops hodgsoni*
* *Saigs talarica*
* *Nemorhaedus cranbrooki*
* *Nemorhaedus goral*

* *Capricornis crispus*
* *Capricornis sumatraensis*
* *Budorcas taxicolor*
* *Hemitragus jemlahicus*
* *Capra ibex*
* *Pseudois nayaur*
* *Pseudois schaeferi*
* *Ovis ammon*
* *Bos frontalis*
  （semi-domesticated species）

ARTIODACTYLA

Bos gaurus Gaur

Description Head and body 250 – 330 cm, tail 70 – 105 cm, shoulder height 165 – 220 cm, and weight 650 – 1000 kg. Males are larger than females. Both sexes have horns. In males there is a distinctive hump over the shoulders. The general color is dull brown to blackish brown. The legs below the ankles are white.

Habits Inhabits forested hills and sparse grass steppes near water sources below 1800 m. Active by day, live in herds of 8 – 11 individuals with only 1 mature male. Other males usually are solitary or gather into bachelor groups.

Reproduction Mating occurs throughout the year, but the peak occurs in spring. The gestation period is 270 – 280 days, births take place in December and January. Normally a single calf is born, rarely twins. The young reach sexual maturity in their second year or third year of life. Life span up to 26 years and 2 months in captivity.

Distribution Southern Yunnan. Very rare.

Conservation China: I; CITES: appendix I.

Bos frontalis Mithan

Brief description A domestic form of gaur, it is different from the wild gaur by having shorter legs and males have no dorsal hump. The head is short and the horns grow straight upward.

Bos javanicus Banteng

Brief description Weight 500 – 900kg. The coat is bluish black. Inhabits open areas. They are nocturnal and gregarious. Mating occurs in May to June. Found in adjacent areas of Yunnan and Myanmar.

Bos gaurus

Bos frontalis

Bos grunniens Yak

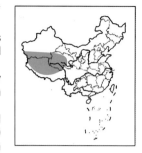

Description Shoulder height 203 cm, males weigh 821 kg and females 306 kg. The wild yak is much larger than the domestic yak. The shoulder hump is distinctive. The body is covered with long, coarse blackish brown hair. The underfur is dense.

Habits Inhabits alpine meadows and cold deserts at altitudes of up to 4000 – 6000 m. The females and young congregate in herds of several dozen. The males usually solitary or in small groups of 2 – 3. Grazes at night or in the early morning. Feeds on various type of food including mosse, but mainly feeds on grass.

Reproduction Mating occurs in September. The gestation period is 258 days, birth occurs in May and June, the females give birth to 1 calf every 2 years. The maximum longevity is 25 years.

Distribution Qingzang plateau, there are several hundred thousand in the wild.

Conservation China: I; IUCN VU; CITES; appendix I.

Gazella subgutturosa Goitred gazelle

Description Head and body 88 – 109 cm, tail 12 – 18 cm, and weight 28 – 42 kg. The males have horns and have swollen throats during the rutting season. The tail back is brownish black.

Habits Inhabits deserts and semi-deserts. Usually in herds of 2 – 6 individuals. The males live alone or live in small groups. They are most active at day. When the animal is in motion the tail wags vertically. Feeds mostly on grasses, but also eats leaves of shrubs.

Reproduction Mating occurs in winter. Gestation lasts about 6 months and produce 1 or 2 young from May to June.

Distribution North China, and northwest China. An estimated of several hundred thousand individuals in the wild.

Conservation China: II.

Gazella subgutturosa

Bos grunnieus

ARTIODACTYLA

Pantholops hodgsoni Tibetan antelope

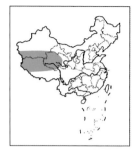

Description Head and body 130 – 140 cm, tail about 10 cm, shoulder height 79 – 94 cm, and weight 25 – 50 kg. The males have horns, which are slim and straight almost vertical to the head, 51 – 71 cm long, and are strongly ridged. The coat is short, dense and woolly. The back and sides are pale reddish brown. In males the head is dull brown or black. The underparts of the body, tail, innersides of the limbs and throat are white or grayish white.

Habits Inhabits open plateau areas at elevations of 3400 – 5500 m. When males are walking, the heads are held high. Active mostly in the morning and in the evening. They are gregarious, usually about 10 in a herb. Male herds contain 2 – 5 individuals. Feeds on grasses and tender leaves of low bushes.

Reproduction Mating begins in winter. The gestation period is about 6 months. Once a year, a single is born.

Distribution Mainly distribute in Qingzang plateau, an endemic species of China. An estimated of 100 thousand individuals in the wild.

Conservation China: I; IUCN: VU; CITES: appendix I.

Procapra picticaudata Tibetan gazelle

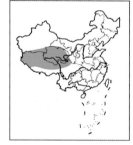

Description Head and body 91 – 105 cm, tail 2 – 10 cm, shoulder height 54 – 64 cm, and weight 20 – 35 kg. The males have curved backward deflection horns. The body is brown. The rump patch, underparts and innersides of the limbs are white. The tail back is brown.

Habits Inhabits plateaus, steppes, alpine meadows, deserts, and semi-deserts. Usually 3 – 5 individuals in a herd. In winter they gather in groups of about 30 individuals. During the summer are active in the morning and evening. Wander while grazing. In the winter migrate to valleys. Feeds on grass.

Reproduction Mating mainly occurs from December to January. Duration of gestation is 6 months. Births take place in June and August with 1 offspring, occasionally 2. Reach sexual maturity in the third years of life.

Distribution Mainly distributed in Xizang and the Northwest plateau. Estimated to be several hundred thousand in the wild.

Conservation China: II.

Pantholops hodgsoni

Procapra picticaudata

Procapra gutturosa Mongolian gazelle

Description Head and body 110 – 148 cm, tail 5 – 12 cm, shoulder height 54 – 84 cm, and weight 25 – 45 kg. Only the males have horns. The body color is brownish yellow. The rump patch is white.

Habits Inhabits arid hilly grasslands and hemieremion pedium areas. Active in the morning and evening. Feeds on grass. They are gregarious, and live in herds of more than 10 individuals. Before the mating season they form large migratory herds of thousands. In late spring and in early summer the migratory herds split into small male and female herds.

Reproduction Mating occurs from December to January. The duration of gestation is about 6 months. The females produce 2 young, occasionally 3, rarely 1. The young reach sexual maturity in the second year of life.

Distribution Eastern part of Nei Mongol. An estimated of 200 000 – 300 000 in winter.

Conservation China: II.

Procapra przewalskii

Przewalski's gazelle

Description Head and body about 100 cm, tail 7 – 10 cm, and weight 21 – 32 kg. The body is yellowish brown with white rump patch. Only the males have horns and the points are curve inward and turned to form a hook.

Habits Inhabits plains, mountain valleys and around lakes of semi desert areas. It lives in small herds of a few individuals to a dozen individuals. In winter, it forms large herds. Feeds mainly on sedges, grass and other sandy plants.

Reproduction Mating occurs in winter and produces 1 young from May to June.

Distribution The Przewalski's gazelle is extinct in Nei Mongol, Ningxia, and Gansu, but according to the 1996 survey it still exists on the northern shores of Qinghai Lake with 2 isolated low population of about 300.

Conservation China: I; IUCN: CR.

Procapra gutturosa

Procapra przewalskii

Saiga tatarica Saiga

Description Head and body 108 – 146 cm, tail 7 – 10 cm, shoulder height 60 – 80 cm, and weight 32 – 51 kg. Females are smaller than males. The head is large. The winter coat is heavy, dense and woolly. The body is grayish white. The males have translucent pale amber horns. It has a short proboscislike nose with a high nose bridge.

Habits Inhabits rugged and hard ground areas of semi-deserts. They are fast runners, but are unable to jump. Grazes in the morning and in the evening. Feeds on various kinds of drought resistance plants.

Reproduction Mating occurs in winter. Gestation lasts 139 – 153 days. The females give birth to 1 or 2 young. The young become sexually mature at 1.5 years. Maximum life span is 10 – 12 years.

Distribution Steppe areas of northern Xinjiang. Extinct in the wild.

Conservation China: I; IUCN: VU.

Capricornis sumatraensis

Mainland serow

Description Head and body 140 – 180 cm, tail 8 – 16 cm, shoulder height 85 – 94 cm, and weight 50 – 140 kg. Both males and females have short and pointed horns, the points are smooth. A mane runs from the neck to the withers. The body is dark gray or black.

Habits Inhabits rocky or rugged mountains covered with dense forest in subtropical regions. It is most active in the morning and in the evening. The serow lives alone. Feeds on weeds, leaves of woody plants.

Reproduction Mating occurs from autumn to winter. Gestation lasts about 7 months, birthing in May to June. Sexually mature at 1.5 years. Captives have lived for more than 10 years.

Distribution South of Qinlin Mts. range.

Conservation China: II IUCN: VU; CITES: appendix I.

Saiga tatarica

Capricornis sumatraensis

ARTIODACTYLA

Capricornis crispus Taiwan serow

Description Head and body only 80 – 114 cm, the tail is very short. The coat is short and not bushy. Body color blackish brown. The dorsal ridge is black, the chin, throat and back of the neck have brownish yellow spots. Both sexes have sharp horns, that curve slightly backward.

Habits Inhabits rugged and steep rock faces of mountains at altitudes of 1000 – 3000 m. It is solitary. Most active in the early morning and at night. Feeds on tender plant leaves and twigs.

Reproduction Mating occurs in October and November. Gestation lasts about 7 months, the female gives birth to 1 young.

Distribution Primary forest of Taiwan. Rare.

Conservation China: I; IUCN: VU.

Nemorhaedus goral Common goral

Description Head and body 106 – 130 cm, tail 12 – 20 cm, shoulder height 50 – 78cm, and weight 22 – 30 kg. Resembles goats, but do not have beards. Both sexes have horns. The coat is grayish brown. There is a short black mane on the neck that extends backward to form a dorsal stripe.

Habits Inhabits mountain forests. The gorals live in pairs or in small groups of 3 – 5 individuals. They are active in the morning and in the evening. Feeds on tender leaves and twigs of shrubs and grass.

Reproduction. Mating occurs from autumn to winter. Gives birth to 1 young, rarely 2 in May and June. Lactation lasts about 4 months, the young are sexually mature in the second year. Life span in captivity is 17.5 years.

Distribution Northeast China, southwest China forested areas. Estimated numbers at more than 10 thousand.

Conservation China: II; IUCN: VU; CITES: appendix I.

Capricornis crispus

Nemorhaedus goral

Nemorhaedus cranbrooki Red goral

Description Head and body 93 – 103 cm, tail 10 – 12 cm, shoulder height 57 – 61 cm, and weight 20 – 30 kg. Similar in size to the common goral, but the tail is shorter and the mane is not distinctive. The body is reddish brown, the back is darker and the below paler. Both sexes have black horns that range from 12 – 16 cm in length. The horn are ridged, with smooth points.

Habits Inhabits mountain forests at altitudes of 2000 – 4500 m. In summer they live in meadows and thickets above the timber line. In winter they move to mixed needle and broad leaved forests or grass glade and thickets below the snow line. Active in the early morning and evening, they bed down over night on rock ledge of cliffs. Feeds on lichens, weeds, tender leaves and twigs of shrubs. They live solitarily, but the young live with the mother.

Reproduction Mating occurs around December. The gestation period is 6 months, and givas birth to a single young in June.

Distribution Eastern Xizang and northwest Yunnan. They have a small distribution range and the numbers are low.

Conservation China: I; IUCN: VU.

Nemorhaedus cranbrooki (♂)

A Mother hides with her young in bushes

Budorcas taxicolor `Takin`

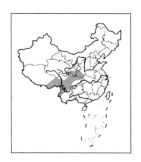

Description Head and body 170 – 320 cm, tail 10 – 15 cm, shoulder height 107 – 140 cm, and weight 300 – 600 kg. Males are larger than females. Body heavily built and oxlike. There is a slight hump at the nose and tufts of long hair protrude from the throat. Both sexes have horns. In the young the horns are slim and straight, but in adults thick at the base which grow outward and than curving backward and upward. The body is brownish yellow, brown or grayish white.

Habits Inhabit high mountain forests at an altitude of 1500 – 4000 m. The takin lives in groups, in small herbs there are 3 – 5 individuals, usually about 20 but may become very large, numbering over a 100. The old males are solitary. Feeds on a wide variety of items, mostly on twigs, and leaves of woody plants and also eats bamboo leaves, grasses, seeds and fruits.

Reproduction Mating occurs in July and August. Gestation lasts 200 – 220 days. The female gives birth to 1 young, which weighs about 11 kg, and follows its mother after three day of birth. Reach sexual maturity in 3.5 years. The life span under natural conditions is 16 – 18 years.

Distribution Qinlin Mts. of Shaanxi, southern Gansu, Sichuan and Xizang.

Conservation China: I; IUCN: VU; CITES: appendix II.

Budorcas taxicolor bedfordi

Budorcas taxicolor tibetana

Hemitragus jemlahicus Himalayan tahr

Description Head and body 130 – 170 cm, tail about 9 cm, shoulder height 62 – 100 cm, and the weight may reach 108 kg in males. Lack a beard but have a long coarse mane around the shoulders. Both sexes have horns. The body is dark brown.

Habits Inhabits rugged mountain forests at altitudes of 3000 – 4000 m. Live in groups of 2 – 20 individuals. Active at dawn and dusk. Feeds mainly on grass and sedge.

Reproduction Mating occurs from October to January. The gestation period is 180 – 242 days and the females give birth to 1 young, sometime 2 from June to July. In captivity the life span is 21 years and 6 months.

Distribution Southern Xizang.

Conservation China: I; IUCN: VU.

Capra ibex Ibex

Description Head and body 115 – 170 cm, tail 10 – 20 cm, shoulder height 65 – 105 cm, and males weigh 80 – 100 kg, females 30 – 50 kg. Both sexes have horns, and may reach 100 cm in males.

Habits Inhabits high rugged rocky mountains or alpine meadows at altitudes of 3000 – 6000m. It does not enter dense forest. Usually lives in groups of 4 – 10 individuals, but sometimes up to several dozen or over a 100 individuals. Active in the morning and evening. Feeds on grasses and weeds.

Reproduction Mating occurs in winter. The gestation period is 147 – 180 days resulting a single, rarely two offspring in May or June. The young become sexually mature at 2 – 3 years of age. Life span 22 years.

Distribution Western Gansu, Nei Mongol and Xinjiang. There are several hundred thousand individuals in Xinjiang, but in the other areas the population is very low.

Conservation China: I.

Hemitragus jemlahicus

Capra ibex

217

ARTIODACTYLA

Pseudois nayaur Blue sheep

Description Head and body 108 – 140 cm, tail 13 – 30 cm, shoulder height 69 – 90 cm, and weight 50 – 74.5 kg in males and for females 45 – 50 kg. Both sexes have horns. The horns in males are larger than females and are up to 82 cm long with a circumference of 28 cm at the base. The winter coat is thick, dense, and brownish gray with a tinge of staty blue. The underparts and innersides of the legs are white, the sides and fronts of the legs have black stripes.

Habits Inhabits plateaus, alpine rocky areas or valley grass plots. The blue sheep are active at day, usually live in groups from a few individuals to over 10, sometimes may form large herds of more than 100. Feeds mainly on grass, but also eats herds, sedge and lichens.

Reproduction Mating occurs in winter. Gestation lasts about 160 days and gives birth to 1 young in May and June. The lactation period is about 6 months. The young reach sexual maturity at 1.5 years of age. Under captivity conditions may live for 24 years.

Distribution Mainly distributed in areas of northwest and southwest China. Now numbering in the hundreds of thousands.

Conservation China: II.

Pseudois nayaur

Ovis ammon Argali

Description Head and body 180 – 200 cm, shoulder height 110 – 125 cm and weight 95 – 140 kg for males, large individuals may exceed to 180 kg. Females are smaller than males. The ears are small, tail short, the coat is long, dense and velvety. Both sexes have horns. In males the horns are thick and up to 100 cm long but may exceed 170 cm. The horns are curved and spiral shaped which rotated at an angle of 360 degree. At the base of the horn is 40 cm in circumference. The horns of females are much smaller and slightly curved. The body color grayish brown with a white rump patch.

Habits Inhabits tree limit plateaus and mountains at elevations of 3000 – 5000 m. They are poor jumpers and often avoid cliffs. They are gregarious, live in groups of 3 – 5 individuals or in herds of several dozen. Feed and rest intermittently throughout the day. Feeds mainly on grasses, but also eats tender leaves and twigs of shrubs.

Reproduction Mating occurs in winter. Gestation lasts 150 – 160 days, gives birth to 1 offspring in May and June. Twins are not rare.

Distribution Qingzang plateau, Nei Mongol. Now over 10 thousand.

Conservation China: II; IUCN: VU; CITES: appendix II.

Ovis ammon

PHOLIDOTA

The pholidota are very specialized mammals. The body is covered with large, flat overlapping scales, which are modified from hair. The belly lacks scales but is well haired. There are a few coarse hairs present between scales and on the belly. The snout is long and narrow, the mouth pikelike, the adults have no teeth. The sharp claws on the forefeet are well developed adapted for digging. This order only contains 1 family with 2 genera and 7 species in the world. China has I genus and I species.

Manis pentadactyla Chinese pangolin

Description Head and body 37 – 48 cm, tail 24 – 34 cm, and weight 2.2 – 3.7 kg.

Habits Inhabits hilly lands, forests or thick bushes especially where the soil is soft. It is solitary and nocturnal, it can climbs trees and swim, it also digs well. When walking the animal walks on its knuckles. When frightened it curls itself into a tight ball which protects the parts, which lack scales, such as the snout, chin, face, throat, belly and inner limbs. Feeds chiefly on termites. It uses its large claws to tear apart termite mounds while the long and sticky tongue flicks in and out of the passage ways to pick out the insects.

Reproduction Mating occurs in autumn. The gestation period is about 140 days, gives birth to 1 young, rarely 2 in early spring. The young rides on its mother's back while she moves around. Under captive conditions the life span is 13.1 years.

Distribution South of Yangzi River.

Conservation China: II; CITES: appendix II.

Manis pentadactyla

Protect behavior of pangolin curing into a ball

223

RODENTIA

The rodents are the most abundant and are distributed worldwide. The major characteristics of rodents are that they have a pair of long and prominent upper and lower incisors, which grow throughout life. There are no canines, therefore a distinct space is found between the incisors and the cheek teeth. There are 27 families, 380 genera and 1739 species in the world. China has 12 families and 185 species.

Sciuridae	29	species
Petauristidae	16	species
Castoridae	1	species
Platacanthomyidae	1	species
Rhozomyidae	4	species
Muridae	44	species
Cricetidae	22	species
Arvicolidae	44	species
Gliridae	2	species
Zapodidae	7	species
Dipodidae	11	species
Hystricidae	3	species
attach: Myocastoridae	1	species

Nuts nibbled by squirrels

Sciuridae

This family includes arboreal and terrestrial squirrels. The tree squirrels have large ears, long legs, the tail is long and will covered with hair. The ground squirrels have small ears, the hind legs are relatively longer than the forelegs, the tail is short and small. All are active during the daytime. Feeds mainly on nuts and plant matter. There are 10 genera and 29 species in China.

* *Sciurus vulgaris*
* *Callosciurus erythraeus*
  Callosciurus finlaysoni
  Callosciurus quinquestriatus
  Callosciurus caniceps
  Callosciurus phayrei
  Callosciurus pygerythrus
  Tamiops macclellandii
* *Tamiops swinhoei*
  Menetes berdmorei
  Dremomys lokriah
  Dremomys gularis
* *Dremomys pernyi*
  Dremomys pyrrhomerus
  Dremomys rufigenis

Ratufa bicolor
* *Sciurotamias davidianus*
  Sciurotamias forresti
* *Tamias sibiricus*
* *Marmota baibacina*
  Marmota bobak
* *Marmota caudata*
* *Marmota himalayana*
* *Spermophilus dauricus*
  Spermophilus major
* *Spermophilus erythrogenys*
  Spermophilus fulvus
  Spermophilus relictus
* *Spermophilus undulatus*

High reproductive rate in rodents

Sciurus vulgaris Eurasian red squirrel

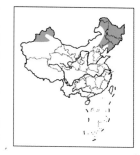

Description Head and body 20 – 24 cm, tail 18 – 21 cm, and weight 260 – 445 g. Body color is blackish brown. The ears are pointed with a long coarse tuft.

Habits Inhabits needle leafed forests or mixed needle and broad leafed forests. Builds its nests in trees hollow or in the branches. Active during the day. Feeds on nuts of pine and hazel, but also eats buds, tender twigs, leaves, berries, insects and other animals. It does not hibernate, but in autumn they store food for winter.

Reproduction Mating occurs in February and March. Gestation lasts 35 – 45 days. There are 2 litters per year each with 4 – 6 young. Attain sexual maturity in 5 – 8 months. Life span is about 8 – 9 years.

Distribution Northeast China and northern Xinjiang.

Callosciurus erythraeus

Red-bellied squirrel

Description Head and body 19 – 24 cm, tail 16 – 22 cm, and weight 280 – 420g. The back is olive yellow, and is reddish brown or chestnut brown underneath, but pale yellow in some individuals.

Habits Inhabits tropical and subtropical forests, but also found in bushes near cultivated lands. It is active during the day. Feeds on a great variety of seeds, tender leaves, fruits, pine and hazel nuts and will sometimes eat bird's eggs, small birds and insects.

Reproduction Mating occurs from March to October. There are 2 litters in a year, each with 2 – 3 young, maximum 5.

Distribution Southern parts of Yangzi River.

Sciurus vulgaris

Callosciurus erythraeus

RODENTIA

Tamiops swinhoie
Swinhoe's striped squirrel

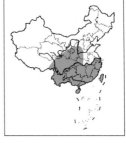

Description Head and body 12 – 14 cm, tail 7 – 11 cm, and weight 66 – 90 g. There are 7 dark and light stripes alternating on the back. The two outermost stripes are sheen in color. The underside is pale yellow.

Habits Inhabits all types of tropical and subtropical forests. It builds its nest in hollows of trees. Active at day. Feeds on tender leaves, pine cones and fruits. It also eats insects.

Reproduction Mating occurs from March to October. Pregnant females are seen in April, gives birth to 1 – 5 young, usually 2 – 3 individuals. Two litters per year.

Distribution Southern parts of Yellow river.

Tamias sibiricus Siberian chipmunk

Description Head and body 15 – 17 cm, tail 10 – 12 cm, and weight about 100 g. There are 5 black strips along the back. The rump is rusty red, underparts flesh colored. They have cheek pouches.

Habits Inhabits mountains, forests and shrublands of plain areas. Lives in crevices, among rocks and hollow trees. Active during day time, mostly on ground, can climb trees and bushes. Feeds mainly on seeds, tender leaves, buds and nuts. It hibernates in late November and emerges in March.

Reproduction Mating occurs from April to September. Gestation lasts 35 – 40 days. There are 1 or 2 litters per year, and each litter has 3 – 6 young. Sexual maturity in 10 month.

Distribution Northeast China. Gansu, Shanxi and Shaanxi.

Tamiops swinhoie

Tamias sibiricus

RODENTIA

Dremomys pernyi
Perny's long-nosed squirrel

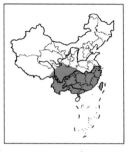

Description Head and body 17 – 20 cm, tail 14 – 17 cm, and weight 160 – 200 g. The snout is long and pointed. Back olive yellow and underparts white. There are white spots behind the ears.

Habits Inhabit ravines or near creaks of tropical and subtropical forests. They are arboreal, but often come to the ground to forage. It builds its nest in trees. Active in the morning and in the evening. Feeds mainly on fruits and insects.

Reproduction Mating occurs in March throughout October. The female gives birth to 2 – 6 young.

Distribution South of Qinlin range, south of Yangzi River and Taiwan.

Sciurotamias davidianus
Père David's rock squirrel

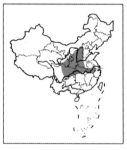

Description Head and body 20 – 23 cm, tail 12 – 14 cm, and weight 220 – 300 g. The back is grayish yellow and belly yellowish pink. The back of the ears have white or pale yellow spots. It has cheek pouches.

Habits Inhabits rocky areas of mountain forest edges. It is a ground dweller. Active during the day, can climb trees and bushes. Builds nests in crevices among rocks. Feeds on nuts and seeds.

Reproduction Mating occurs from March to October. Pregnant females are seen in April through October There are 2 litters a year each with 2 – 3 young .

Distribution Shanxi, Shaanxi, Gansu, Sichuan and Hubei.

Dremomys pernyi

Sciurotamias davidianus

Spermomphilus erythrogenys
Red-cheeked ground squirrel

Description Head and body 18 – 25 cm, tail 3 – 5 cm, and weight 210 – 500 g. The back is sandy yellow or grayish yellow with yellowish white wavy stripes. The front ears and chin are brownish yellow.

Habits Inhabits low mountains, hilly lands, semi-deserts. Live in ground burrows, active during the day. Feeds on green parts of plant material, seeds, roots, tubers, it also eats insects. In early spring it feeds on withered stems and roots. It hibernates in September and emerges in middle of March.

Reproduction It emerges to breed in spring. Annually 1 litter. The gestation period is 25 – 38 days, the female gives birth to 3 – 11 young, usually 5 – 8 young. The young reach sexual maturity in the following spring.

Distribution Xinjiang and north Nei Mongol.

Spermophilus dauricus
Daurian ground squirrel

Description Head and body 16 – 23 cm, tail 5.5 – 7.5 cm, weight 160 – 230 g. The color of the back is dark yellow, the sides and the outersides of the forelegs are sandy yellow.

Habits Inhabits grassland. It is a typical terrestrial grassland squirrel, its most suitable habitat being the droughty desert grasslands. It is solitary and diurnal. Feeds mainly on green parts of plant material, it also eats seeds and insects. Generally, it hibernates in late September and emerges in late March.

Reproduction Mating occurs in April, it breeds once a year. The gestation period is about 28 days and each litter has 5 – 6 young. Life span is about 7 years.

Distribution Northeast and North China.

Spermomphilus erythrogenys

Spermophilus dauricus

233

Spermophilus undulatus
Long-tailed souslik

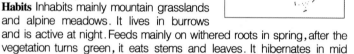

Description Head and body 22 – 28 cm, tail 9 – 14 cm, and weight 250 – 580 g. The coat is yellowish brown on the back with inconspicuous and irregular spotlike stripes, in contrast the stripes on the rump are rather conspicuous.

Habits Inhabits mainly mountain grasslands and alpine meadows. It lives in burrows and is active at night. Feeds mainly on withered roots in spring, after the vegetation turns green, it eats stems and leaves. It hibernates in mid September and emerges in April.

Reproduction Mating occurs after spring emergence. Gestation lasts about 30 days. One litter per year and 3 – 11 young are born, usually 6 – 8. The young reach sexual maturity after wintering.

Distribution Xinjiang, Nei Mongol, and the northern parts of Heilongjiang.

Marmota caudata Long-tailed marmot

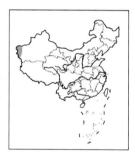

Description Head and body 47 – 53 cm, tail 15 – 20 cm, and weight about 3 – 7 kg. The coat is rusty red or reddish brown – yellow. The tail tip is black.

Habits Inhabits alpine meadows, high rocky mountain valleys and edges of cold deserts at altitudes of 3 200 – 5 000m. It is active during the day and lives in family groups. Feeds mainly on pasture and occasionally on grass seeds and insects. Generally, it hibernates in early September and emerges in mid April.

Reproduction Mating occurs in burrows before they emerge. The gestation period is 30 – 32 days, the female gives birth to 4 – 5 young in May and June. One litter per year. The young are sexual maturity at 2 years of age.

Distribution Western Xinjiang.

Spermophilus undulatus

Marmota caudata

235

Marmota himalayana Himalayan marmot

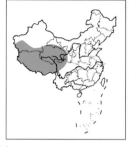

Description Head and body 37 – 40 cm, tail 12 – 13 cm, ears 3 – 4 cm, and weight 4 – 8 kg. The body is stocky and the legs are short with well developed claws adapted for digging. The coat is brownish yellow on the back with thin black stripes. Tail tip is blackish brown.

Habits Inhabits high altitude steppes and alpine meadows at 3000 – 5200 m. They are terrestrial and live in groups. Active during the day. Primarily found on hillsides, foot of the mountains or on slops and valley floors. Feeds on plant leaves and stems, rarely on small animals. Hibernates in winter.

Reproduction Mating occurs right after emerging from hibernation. Pregnant females are seen in late March and young individuals are seen in June. Litter size 4 – 5 individuals.

Distribution Qingzang plateau.

Marmota baibacine Steppe marmot

Description Head and body 38 – 62 cm, tail 10 – 19 cm, and weight 3 – 7.2 kg. The back is sandy yellow or sandy brown, belly and innersides of the legs are brownish yellow. White around the mouth.

Habit Inhabits alpine meadows, dry steppes and montane forests at elevations of 1200 – 3000m. These animals live in family groups. Active during the day. Feeds mainly on green parts of plant matter and some insects. In early spring it digs and eats withered roots. They hibernate from late August or early September and emerge in April.

Reproduction Mating occurs in April. The gestation period is 30 – 40 days, the females produce 1 litter per year with 3 – 10 young. Lactation lasts about 30 day. Become sexual maturity at 3 years of age. Life span is 10 – 13 years.

Distributions Northwest of Xinjiang.

Marmota himalayana

Marmota baibacina

237

RODENTIA

Petauristidae

The characteristics are generally similar with those of rodentia, but in addition the limbs and body sides are connected by a fold of skin (patagium), which forms a broad, fur-covered membrane that enables the squirrels to glide through the air for a distance as far as 10 meters. The tail is long and hairy used in flight as a rudder and to maintain balance. There are 14 genera and about 38 species in the world. China has 7 genera and 15 species The species are given as follows:

* *Petaurista alborufus*
  Petaurista caniceps
  Petaurista elegans
  Petaurista magnificus
  Petaurista pectoralis
  Petaurista petaurista
  Petaurista philippensis
  Petaurista sybilla

* *Petaurista xanthipes*
  Eupetaurus cinereus
  Pteromys volans
  Hylopetes alboniger
  Hylopetes electilis
  Trogopterus xanthipes
  Aeretes melanopterus
  Belomys pearsonii

Petaurista alborufus
Red and white flying squirrel

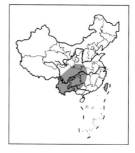

Description Head and body 54 – 58 cm, tail 40 – 44 cm. The Taiwan specimens are smaller, the head and body length is 35 – 43 cm, tail 44 – 48 cm. The back is red, the face and belly white. The tail color same as the back, but darker at the tip.

Habits Inhabits deep valleys of rain forests and tropical mixed broad and needle leaved forests or deciduous broad leaved forests. It is solitary, except during the mating period. It lives in tree hollows, and is active at night. Feeds on young leaves and buds, seeds and fruits.

Reproduction These squirrels have a low reproduction rate. There are 2 litters per year and only 2 individual per litter. Under captive conditions the maximum life span is 14 years and 8 months.

Distribution Southern parts of China including Taiwan.

Petaurista alborufus

Petaurista xanthotis
Chinese giant flying squirrel

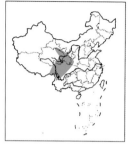

Description Head and body 34 – 40 cm, tail 31 – 36 cm, and weight 730 – 1200 g. The body and patagium are grayish yellow brown or blackish brown. The ears are blackish brown with yellow spots on the back. The tail is long and bushy.

Habits Inhabits needle leaved forests at altitudes of 2000 – 3400 m. It is a typically high mountain type flying squirrel. It is nocturnal. During the day it remains inside a tree hollow by night it emerges to forage. Feeds on tender leaves of plant material, inflorescence, bark, nuts of pine and fir and insects.

Reproduction Embryos are seen in pregnant females caught in April.

Distribution Endemic species of China.

Belomys pearsonii
Hairy-eared flying squirrel

Description Head and body about 18 – 26 cm, tail about 10 – 16 cm. It is a relatively small species. The coat is a mixture of reddish brown and grayish black, the belly pale rust and the patagium is blackish brown. The chestnut brown tail is bushy and slightly spread apart on the two sides. The areas around the eyes are black. The ears are small and have long tufts at the base.

Habits Inhabits tropical and subtropical forests at altitudes of 500 – 2400 m. It is nocturnal. Feeds on leaves and fruits, which contain high concentrations of saccharide.

Distribution Southern parts of China.

Petaurista xanthotis

Belomys pearsonii

241

RODENTIA

Castoridae

The Castotidae are relatively large size rodents. They are semi-aquatic animals. The tail is wide and flattened horizontally, covered with scales and nearly hairless, The hind feet are webbed. There are a pair of castor glands located in front of the anus, which secretes castoreum. There is only 1 genus and 2 species in the world. China has only 1 species.

Castor fiber Eurasian beaver

Description Head and body 60 – 100 cm, tail 21 – 29.5 cm, and weight 17 – 30 kg. The beaver is the largest rodent in China. The head is short and blunt; the eyes small, the ears scarcely visible, almost completely hidden by hair only a little portion is shown. The tail is wide and flat, covered with scales and hairless.

Habits. Inhabits banks of lakes, river, streams where groves of willow, poplar and birch are abundant. Beavers are semi-aquatic mammals, and live in colonies. They are mainly nocturnal, seldom appear by day. Feeds on the twigs, bark of willow and poplar trees, also reeds and weeds.

Reproduction Mating occurs from January to February. Gives birth to 1 litter of 1 – 6 young, usually 2 – 3 young in April and May. Life span 12 – 20 years.

Distribution Northeast parts of Xinjiang. About 500 – 600 individuals in the wild.

Conservation China: I.

View of tail and webbed hind foot of Eurasian beaver

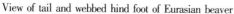

Habitat and cut down trees

Castor fiber

RODENTIA

Muridae

Muridae are small rodents. Their body weight ranges from 12 – 600 g. The tail is long with annulations of scales and sparse short hair. The ears are relatively large. No cheek pouches. They are highly adapted to a wide variety of environments and have high reproductive ability. Some members of this family are commemsal species, living in association with humans, while other murid species are pests to agriculture and forestry. It should be noted that a certain number of serious human diseases can be transmitted from murid species. Muridae are of great value in ecosystem in many terrestrial food chains as primary consumers fed upon by carnivores. There are 457 species in the world. Of these China has 16 families and 44 species. The species are given as follows:

Hapalomys delacouri
Vandeleuria oleracea
Vernaya fulva
* Micromys minutus
Apodemus agrarius
Apodemus chevrieri
* Apodemus draco
Apodemus latronum
Apodemus orestes
Apodemus peninsulae
* Apodemus sylvaticus
Dacnomys millardi
Rattus flavipectus
* Rattus losea
Rattus nitidus
* Rattus norvegicus
Rattus rattus
Rattus turkestanicus
Maxomys exulans
Maxomys rajah
Maxomys surifer
Maxomys musschenbroekii

Niviventer andersoni
Niviventer brahma
Niviventer confucianus
Niviventer coninga
Niviventer cremoriventer
Niviventer eha
Niviventer excelsior
Niviventer fulvescens
Berylmys berdmorei
Berylmys manipulus
Berylmys bowersi
Leopoldamys edwardsi
Chiromyscus chiropus
Hadromys humei
Mus caroli
Mus cookii
Mus musculus
Mus pahari
* Bandicota indica
Nesokia indica
Chiropodomys gliroides
Chiropodomys jingdongensis

Apodemus draco Chinese field mouse

Description Head and body 7 – 10 cm, tail 7 – 10 cm, and weight 12 – 27 g. The tail is about equal to the head and body length. Dorsally the body and tail are grayish brown and the underparts are grayish white.

Habits Inhabits forests, bamboo stands, shrublands, grasslands at altitudes below 3500 m. Builds its nest in hollows of trees or in the grass. It is active at night. Feeds on fruits and seeds, also takes greenery and insects.

Reproduction Mating occurs from March to September. The females produce 2 litters a year, gives each birth to 2 – 3 young.

Distribution Southern Yangzi River.

Apodemus sylvaticus Wood mouse

Description Head and body 8 – 11 cm, tail 7 – 9 cm, and weight 30 – 40 g. The body coloration is distinctly bicolored. The back is sandy brown or grayish brown and the belly white which are noticeable on the sides of the body. The tail is also bicolored. The back is grayish brown and under side grayish white.

Habits Inhabits alpine meadows, and steppes at altitudes below 3800 m, it is also found in desert plains. Prefers forest edges, grass glades, valley shrubslands, forest clearings and stone piles. It is active at night. Feeds on various kinds of plant seeds, it also eats twigs and leaves and Insects.

Reproduction Mating occurs from spring to autumn. It can have up to 2 – 4 litters in a year, each litter consisting of 3 – 9 young.

Distribution Western and north Xinjiang and west of Xizang.

Apodemus draco

Apodemus sylvaticus

Rattus norvegicus Norway rat

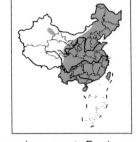

Description Head and body 13 – 21 cm, tail 10 – 17 cm, and weight 95 – 320 g. The color is grayish brown on the back and grayish white underneath. The feet are grayish white.

Habits Inhabits urban areas. This species is commensal with human beings. Its favorite haunts are sewers, rubbish piles, garbage dumps, dock areas, farmyards and cultatived areas. It is a colonial, nocturnal and omnivorous rat. Feeds on cereals, meat, snails, crabs, small fish and insects.

Reproduction Reproduction rate is high, may produce 3 – 8 litters per year. In subtropical areas, usually there are spring, summer and autumn breeding peaks. In tropical areas it breeds throughout the year. The estrous cycle is 4 – 6 days, the gestation period is 21 – 26 days, bears 6 – 9 young in each litter. The young are sexual maturity in 2 – 3 months.

Distribution Throughout China.

Rattus losea Lesser rice field rat

Description Head and body 12 – 18 cm, tail 12 – 17.5 cm, and weight 60 – 145 g. The coat is yellowish brown or brown on the back, body sides paler and grayish white underneath.

Habits Inhabits fields, creek sides, graves, stone piles, mud humps and in weeds. Build its nest among rock piles. Nocturnal, but it is most active at dusk. Feeds on cereals seeds, roots, rhizomes, melons, fruits, green parts of vegetation and insects.

Reproduction Reproduces all year around. The females bear more than 3 litters a year, each with 3 – 7 young after a gestation period of 21 – 22 days.

Distribution Zhejiang, Fujian, Taiwan, Guangdong, Guangxi, Hainan and coastal islets.

Rattus norvegicus

Rattus losea

Bandicota indica Greater bandicoot rat

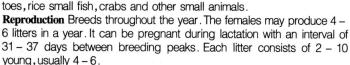

Description Head and body 22 – 28 cm, tail 18 – 25 cm, and weight 500 – 700 g. The coat is long and stiff about 4 cm long. Body color tan to yellowish brown with blackish brown mane down the middle of the back. The rump is covered with long black hair.

Habits Inhabits moist areas near water where the soil is soft. It is usually active at night. Feeds on sugar cane, sweat potatoes, rice small fish, crabs and other small animals.

Reproduction Breeds throughout the year. The females may produce 4 – 6 litters in a year. It can be pregnant during lactation with an interval of 31 – 37 days between breeding peaks. Each litter consists of 2 – 10 young, usually 4 – 6.

Distribution Yunnan, Guangxi, Guangdong and Taiwan.

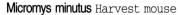

Micromys minutus Harvest mouse

Description Head and body 6 – 7 cm, tail 6 – 8 cm, and weight 5 – 11 g. The tail of this mouse is longer than the head and body length and almost hairless at the end. The coat is brownish yellow and white on the underside.

Habit Inhabits slops of hillylands. It prefers environments of paddy and wheat fields, forest edges, or thick growths of grass. It is active both day and night, but it is most active during night. It builds distinctive, compactly woven globular nests on the wheat stalks and beard grass stems from wither grass and leaves. Feeds mostly on plant seeds, fruits, stems, and sometimes insects.

Reproduction In tropical areas, except in the winter, pregnant females are found in all months. The gestation period is 17 – 18 days. It produces 2 – 5 litters and there are 3 – 10 young in each litter. Sexual maturity in 35 – 40 days. The life span is 16 – 18 months.

Distribution Northeast China, eastern China and southern China.

Bandicota indica

Micromys minutus

RODENTIA

Cricetidae

Small sized rodents. The tails are short with no distinct scales. There are cheek pouches. Creicetidae are found in a wide variety of habitats, including steppes, droughty grasslands, meadows, high mountains, hilllands, deserts, and semi-deserts. There are 7 genera and 22 species in China.

Cricetus cricetus
Phodopus roborovskii
* Phodopus sungorus
Cricetulus barabensis
Cricetulus eversmanni
Cricetulus curtatus
Cricetulus kamensis
Cricetulus longicaudatus
* Cricetulus migratorius
Cricetulus triton
Myospalax aspalax

* Myospalax fontanierii
Myospalax psilurus
Myospalax rothschildi
Myospalax smithi
Meriones chengi
* Meriones libycus
* Meriones meridianus
Meriones tamariscinus
* Meriones unguiculatus
Brachiones przewalskii
* Rhombomys opimus

Cricetulus migratosius Gray hamster

Description Head and body 10 – 12 cm, tail 2.6 – 3.5 cm, and weight 30 – 46 g. The pelage on the back is gray or sandy yellow or brownish yellow with no dorsal strip on the back. The undersides and tail are white.

Habits Inhabits deserts semi-deserts, hilly lands, grasslands, cultivated lands and alpine meadows at altitudes above 3000 m. It also inhabits buildings of cities and towns. They are active both day and night, being most active at night. Feeds on wild plants and seed crops. They also eats mollusks and insects. It has a habit of storing food for future use.

Reproduction Mating occurs in spring. Females produce 2 – 4 litters in a year, each litter has 5 – 8 young. The young that are born in early spring and early summer soon reach sexual maturity and may breed in autumn.

Distribution Xinjiang, Qinghai and western Nei Mongol.

252

Cricetulus migratosius

Cricetulus barabensis Striped hamster

Description Head and body 8 – 12 cm, tail 1.6 – 3.5 cm, and weight 19 – 41 g. The body has distinctive coloring. The back is grayish yellow brown to reddish brown with a black dorsal strip running down the body. The belly is white.

Habits Inhabits deserts, semi-deserts, alpine meadows, versants and cultivated fields. They are nocturnal and burrow dwellers. Feeds on a variety of weed seeds and crops, occasionally prey on insects. Do not hibernate in winter, but store food for winter use.

Reproduction Mating occurs in spring. The gestation period is 17 – 22 days and females produce 3 – 5 litters a year, each with 4 – 8 young, the largest is 10. The young are mature sexually in 2 months.

Distribution Northeast and north China.

Rhombomys opimus Great gerbil

Description Head and body 15 – 17 cm, tail 13 – 16 cm. The coat is sandy yellow on the back and the belly dirty white. The tail is thick and hairy with long black hair at the tip.

Habits Inhabits sand dunes of desert steppes. It is nocturnal and gregarious. Feeds on green vegetation including the roots and stems of forbs.

Reproduction Mating occurs from March to April. The gestation period is 23 – 32 days and the females produce 2 – 3 litters per year. Litter size 1 – 11 young, but usually 4 – 7 young. The young become sexual maturity at 3 – 4 months of age. The life span for females is 3 – 4 year and for males 2 – 3 years.

Distribution North Xinjiang and western Nei Mongol.

Cricetulus barabensis

Rhombomys opimus

Meriones libycus `Libyan jird`

Description Head and body 13 – 17 cm, tail 12.5 – 16.5 cm. The back is grayish brown, the undersides and innersides of the legs are white. The tail brownish yellow with a tuft of black hairs at the end.

Habits Inhabits desert steppes but avoids desert environments, they prefer oasis and often found near farmhouses. It is nocturnal and lives in burrows, in winter they are active under the snow. Feeds on seeds of herds and psammophyte. In spring after the vegetation turns green it takes greenery.

Reproduction Mating occurs in April. Birth takes place in May. Produce two or more litters per year. Gestation lasts about 25 days and 5 – 8 young are born. The offspring that are born in the early spring become sexual maturity in late summer.

Distribution Xinjiang.

Meriones meridianus `Mid-day gerbil`

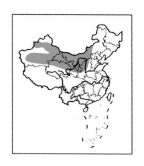

Description Head and body 11 – 14 cm, tail 914 cm and weight 48 – 85 g. The back is sandy yellow in color and the undersides pure white. The tail is rust yellow with a black end.

Habits Inhabits shrubs, sand dunes of deserts, grasslands and cultivated fields. It lives in burrows, and is active at night and in the early morning. Feeds on plants, seeds and insects. It does not hibernate but of stores food in autumn.

Reproduction Mating occurs from March to October. Females produce 2 – 3 litters in a year. The gestation period is 19 – 21 days. Litter size is 3 – 10, usually 5 – 6 young. The young that are born in spring, reach sexual maturity at 65 – 85 days and are able to breed in autumn. The offspring of an autumn litter reach sexual maturity the following spring. In nature the life span is only 3 – 4 months.

Distribution Northwest and north China.

Meriones libycus

Meriones meridianus

Meriones unguiculatus Mongolian gerbil

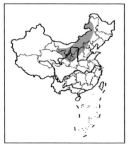

Description Head and body 11 – 13.5 cm, tail 8.5 – 10 cm, and weight 48 – 85 g. The back is brownish gray and the belly is white. The tail is bicolored with the upper surface black and underside brownish yellow.

Habits Inhabits sandy semi-deserts, dry steppes, hillsides, and cultivated fields. The gerbil live in burrows and is active during the day. Feeds on tender leaves and buds in spring and plant seeds during autumn. It does not hibernate in winter, but stores food.

Reproduction Pregnant females are seen throughout the year and produce 3 – 4 litters in a year. Litter size 5 – 6 young, up to 11 or 12. The offspring of the spring litter are capable to breed in autumn.

Distribution Nei Mongol, Gansu and northern Shannxi.

Myospalax fontanierii

Common Chinese zokor

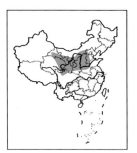

Description Head and body 15 – 26 cm, tail 4 – 6 cm, and weight 200 – 450 g. The body is stocky, the snout short, and there are no external ears. The claws on the forefeet are well developed. The back is pale brown and the belly paler. The tail is sparsely haired.

Habits Inhabits steppes, high mountains and cultivated areas. The zokor has a complicated burrow system. Feeds on subterranean roots and on stems. It does not hibernate, but stores food.

Reproduction Mating occurs from March to April. Annually 1 litter, gives birth to 1 – 5 young, usually 2 – 3 young in May and June.

Distribution Hubei, Shanxi, Shandong, Qinghai, Gansu and Shaanxi.

Meriones unguiculatus

Myospalax fontanierii

Platacanthomyidae

This family is chraracterlized by having a long tail which is about 50% longer then the head and body. The tail has ring scales with a tuft of hair at the end. There are only 2 genera and 2 species, of these 1 genus and 1 species occurs in China.

Typhlomys cinereus
Chinese pygmy dormouse

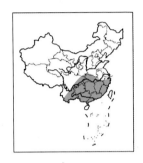

Description Head and body 7.2 – 11.7 cm, tail 10 – 13.8 cm, and weight 17.5 – 32 g. The eyes are small, the external ears are large. The pelage is dense and soft, brownish gray on the back and the underparts pale gray. The tail is dark brown. At the tail base the hair is short and the ring scales are visible. The tip of the tail has long white hair.

Habits Inhabits shady and moist subtropical forests at altitudes of 360 – 1570 m. It lives in burrows near streams, crevices and among rocks. Feeds on leaves, stems, seeds and fruits.

Reproduction Little is know about its reproduction. In a study in Zhejiang 2 pregnant females each with 2 embryos were found in March to May. In Guizhou 5 females were caught from late April to early May of these 3 were lactating and 1 female had 3 embryos. Females caught in Anhui in December had 4 embryos.

Distribution South of Qinlin Mts. range and southern Yangzi River. The habitats are very limited and the population low.

Typhlomys cinereus

Rhizomyidae

Medium sized mammals with stocky bodies. The snout is short, the eyes are small and the external ears are not distinctive. The forehands and claws are well developed adapted for digging. There are 3 genera and 6 species, of these 1 genus and 4 species occur in China.

* * *Rhizomys pruinosus*   *Rhizoimys sumatrensis*
    Rhizomys sinensis   *Cannomys badius*

Rhizomys pruinosus Hoary bamboo rat

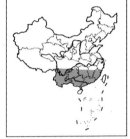

Description Head and tail 30 – 39 cm, tail 13 – 17 cm, and weight 1500 – 2500 g. The overall body is grayish brown with white tips on the guard hairs that give a frosted appearances to the body. The tail is nearly hairless.

Habits Inhabits bamboo thickets or bunch beard grass. They are burrow dwellers. Seldom come up to the ground, and spend much of their life underground. The components of the diet varies geographically. Feeds mainly on bamboo in Sichuan; In Yunnan feeds chiefly on bamboo and subterraneous roots. In Fujian and Jiangxi feeds on beard grass stalks and subterraneous roots.

Reproduction Mating occurs from April to September. Produce 1 – 4 young per litter.

Distribution South of Yangzi River.

Rhizomys pruinosus

Rhizomus sinersis Chinese bamboo rat

Brief description Head and body 25 – 29 cm, tail length 5 – 7cm, and weight 500 – 1300 g. The back is brownish gray and the guard hairs are not tipped white. Inhabits thin bamboo thickets and bunch beard grass. It lives in subterranean burrows. Breeds in spring and again in autumn and each litter has 1 – 5 young.

Distribution South of Qinlin Mts. range.

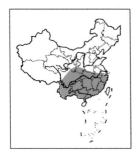

Rhizomus sinersis

Arvicolidae

Most members of this family are small. The body weight is usually less than 100g Their bodies are stocky and in most species the tail is short, which is less than half of the head and body length. The eyes and ears are small. The animals chiefly live in burrows dug underground. There are about 100 species in the world and China has 11 genera and 45 species.

Myopus schisticolor
Clethrionomys frater
Clethrionomys rufocanus
Clethrionomys rutilus
Eothenomys cachinus
Eothenomys chinensis
Eothenomys custos
Eothenomys melanogaster
Eothenomys miletus
Eothenomys olitor
Eothenomys proditor
Eothenomys eva
Eothenomys inez
Alticola argentatus
Alticola macrotis
Alticola roylei
Alticola stoliczkanus
Alticola stracheyi
Alticola strelzowi
Arvicola terrestris
* Ondatra zibethicus
Pitymys irene

Pitymys juldaschi
Pitymys leucurus
Pitymys sikimensis
Proedromys bedfordi
Microtus agrestis
* Microtus arvalis
Microtus brandtii
Microtus clarkei
Microtus fortis
Microtus fuscus
Microtus gregalis
Microtus ilaeus
* Microtus kikuchii
Microtus mandarinus
Microtus maximowiczii
Microtus millicens
Microtus mongolicus
Microtus oeconomus
Microtus socialis
Ellobius talpinus
* Lagurus lagurus
Lagurus luteus

Ondatra zibethicus Muskrat

Description Head and body 23 – 35 cm, tail 20 – 28 cm, and weight 400 – 1000 g. The muskrat is the largest species of Arvicolidae. The pelage is brown to dull brown. Tail scaly flatten at the sides.

Habits Inhabits rivers, lakes, marshlands, swamps, and shallow water areas where aquatic plant is abundant. It is semi-aquatic, lives in burrows along the banks. Active in the morning and evening. Feeds mainly on reeds and aquatic plants, but also some small animals.

Reproduction Mating occurs from May to August. Gestation lasts about 25 days. The females produce 3 – 6 litters in a year, each litter has 6 – 7 young. Reach sexual maturity at 2 months of age. Life span 3 years in nature.

Distribution The muskrat was originally from North America. It was introduced and dispersed in China and has established populations in some areas.

lagurus lagurus Steppe lemming

Description Head and body 9.5 – 12 cm, tail about 1 cm, and weight 15 – 25 g. The back is grayish yellow and the underparts grayish white. There is a black dorsal stripe running from the head to the tail.

Habits Inhabits steppes, and desert steppes, but avoids extreme dry deserts. They are gregarious, live in underground burrows and active at night. It does not hibernate. In winter they forage beneath the snow. Feeds mainly on leaves and stems of pastures.

Reproduction Mating occurs from March to September. The females are in estrous within 24 hours after labor and produce more than 5 litters a year. Each litter contains an average of 8.1 young, which reach sexual maturity at 60 – 75 days.

Distribution Northern Xinjiang.

Ondatra zibethicus

Lagurus lagurus

Microtus arvalis Common vole

Description Head and body 9.6 – 13 cm, tail 3.2 – 4.6 cm, and weight 35 – 50 g. Yellowish brown to dark brown above and the underparts are grayish white.

Habits Inhabits steppes and avoids dry desert environments. It is a typical steppe animal. In summer the animal invades cultivated lands. They are gregarious and live in burrows. Feeds on green parts of leguminous and herbaceous plants. It builds nests and forage beneath the snow in winter. It does not hibernate but stores dry grass in its burrows.

Reproduction Mating occurs in April. The young are born in May. The gestation period is 19 – 25 days, and produce 4 – 5 litters in a year. Each litter has 3 – 6 young. The young females reach sexual maturity in 25 days and males at 45 day. Under natural conditions the life span is less than 1 month, but some individuals may live for up to 1 year.

Distribution Northeast China and Xinjiang.

Microtus kikuchii Taiwan vole

Description Head and body 10 – 13 cm, tail 6 – 10 cm, the tail is longer than half of its body length. The pelage is dull reddish brown above and beneath is nearly white. The ears are short and almost completely covered with fur.

Habits Inhabits grasslands, wilderness, high mountains, shrublands, secondary forests, and forest edges at altitudes of 2000 m in Taiwan. Feeds on seeds, young leaves, buds, and bark.

Reproduction Breeds throughout the year.

Distribution Taiwan.

Microtus arvalis

Microtus kikuchii

Gliridae

Most species are small to medium sized mammals. They are mainly arboreal and a few are terrestrial. The body shape looks like squirrels and resembles rodents. The tail usually is longer or almost equal to the body length. The tail of arboreal species have dense and long fur, as for terrestrial species they have short and sparsely hair on the tail. There are 14 genera and 97 species in the world, of these China has only 2 genera with 2 species.

* *Dryomys nitedula*　　　　　　*Chactocauda sichuanensis*

Dryomys nitedula Forest dormouse

Description Head and body 8 – 10 cm, tail 8 – 10 cm. The tail hair is dense and bushy, especially long on the sides, but the hair on back and ventral sides are short. The back is brownish gray.

Habits Inhabits mountain valleys at latitudes below 2000 m. It builds its nest with branches and leaves, hanging from branches or uses bird's nest. It sleeps through the days and leave the nest at night. Feeds on seeds, and berries but also takes small birds and bird's eggs. It hibernates in the winter.

Reproduction Mating extends from March to August. Gestation lasts about 1 months. Annually it bears 1 litter with 2 – 5 young, occasionally up to 7. Sexual maturity the second year of life.

Distribution Tianshan Mts. range of Xinjiang.

Dryomys nitedula

Zapodidae

A small sized rodent, in appearance it somewhat resembles the house mouse. It has a long tail that is distinctively longer than the head and body length, the hair on the tail is short and sparse with conspicuous scales. There are 4 genera and 17 species in the world, of these 2 genera and 7 species are distributed in China.

Sicista betulina
Sicista caudata
Sicista concolor
Sicista pseudonapaea

Sicista subtilis
* *Sicista tianschanicas*
Eozapus setchuanus

Sicista tianschanicus

Tian shan birch mouse

Description Head and body 5 – 7 cm, tail 8 – 11 cm. The tail is 1.5 times longer than the head and body length. The pelage is grayish brown.

Habits Inhabits mountain steppes, alpine meadows, forest clearings, shrublands and bunchgrass below the spruce forest zone. They are active both day and night, builds its nest in burrows under tree roots or under fallen trees. They hibernate in winter.

Reproduction Produce 1 litter per year. The gestation period is 4 – 5 weeks. Pregnant females caught in Xinjiang in July contained 3 embryos. The young become sexual maturity in the second year of life. The life span is 3 – 4 years.

Distribution Western Tianshan Mts. of Xinjiang.

Sicista tianschanicus

269

Eozapus setchuanus

Sichuan jumping mouse

Brief description Head and body 7 – 8 cm, tail 11 – 13 cm, and weight 15 – 19 g. The pelage is entirely rust brown. The tail is slender. Inhabits shrub lands, meadows, and steppes. They are active at night. Feeds on stems, leaves and seeds.

Distribution Gansu, Ningxia, Shaanxi, Sichuan and Qinghai.

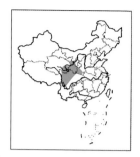

Dipodidae

The dipodidae family are characterized by a series of specializations and adaptations for jumping on sandy soils. The body is usually sandy color. The snout is wide and blunt that ends in a round disk, like a pig's snout. The nostrils have a mobile skin fold to prevent the sand from entering. The eyes and ears are relatively large. The proximal portion of the ear is tubular at the base. The forelegs are small and the hind legs are well developed. The length of the hind legs is at least 3 times longer than the forelegs. They are good jumpers. The tail is longer than the head and body length. In most species, the tail tip has alternating rings of white and black. There are 10 genera and about 30 species in the world. China has 6 genera and 11 species.

* *Dipus sagitta*
  Allactaga bullata
  Allactaga elater
* *Alactagulus sibirica*
  Alactagulus pumilio

  Cardiocranius paradoxus
* *Salpingotus crassicauda*
  Salpingotus kozlovi
  Stylodipus andrewsi
  Stylodipus telum
  Echoreutes naso

Dipus sagitta
Northern three-toed jerboa

Description Head and body 10 – 15 cm, tail 14.5 – 16.5 cm, ears about 2 cm, and weight 60 – 100 g. There are 5 toes on the front foot and 3 on the hind foot. The color is dark yellow or sandy yellow on the back and the belly pure white. The tail has a white tip.

Habits Inhabits plateaus at altitudes of 1000 – 1300 m. They are active during the night. Feeds on roots, tender leaves and seeds, but occasionally insects are also eaten. Hibernate for 6 months from late September and emerges in early April.

Reproduction Mating occurs from April to September with a peak in March and May. Gestation lasts 25 – 30 days, the females produce 2 – 3 litters a year. Each litter contains 1 – 8 young, usually 3 – 4 young.

Distribution Xinjiang, Nei Mongol and north of Shaanxi.

Dipus sagitta

271

RODENTIA

Allactaga sibirica
Mongolian five-toed jerboa

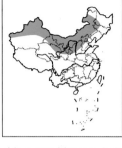

Description Head and body 13 – 15 cm, tail 20 cm, ears about 4 cm, and weight 95 – 140 g. There are 5 toes on each hind foot, of these the third middle toe is well developed. The back is brownish yellow and the underside white. The tail tip is white with black rings.

Habits Inhabits desert steppes, occasionally enters cultivated lands. It is active at night, and is a good jumper, being able to cover up to 2 – 3 m in a single jump. Feeds on roots, stems and leaves and also eats insects. It hibernates in the winter.

Reproduction Mating extends from April to August. Produce 2 – 3 litters annually of 3 – 5 young each.

Distribution North Xinjiang, Nei Mongol, Gansu and Ningxia.

Salpingotus crassicauda
Thick-tailed pygmy jerboa

Description Head and tail 4 – 5 cm, tail about 10 cm, and weight 10 – 14 g. The hind feet has 3 toes concealed by hair. Tail is thick at the base and gradually becomes thin at the tip. The coat is sandy yellow on the back and the belly white.

Habits Inhabits mountain deserts, semi-shrublands, and semi fixed dunes. It is active at night. Feeds on plant matter and also eats insects, spiders and small animals.

Reproduction Mating peak occurs from May to July. Annually 1 litter with 2 – 3 young which become sexual maturity in the second year.

Distribution Northern Xinjiang, western Nei Mongol and north of Ningxia. very rare.

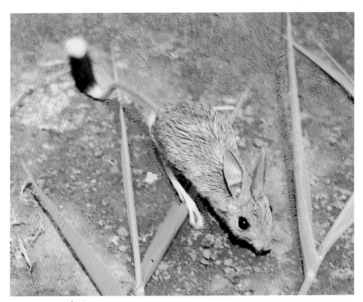

Allactaga sibirica

Salpingotus crassicauda

Hystricidae

Members of this family are stocky and relatively large. The body and tail are covered with long, hard spines. There are 3 genera and 11 species in the world. China has 2 genera and 3 species.

Atherurus macrourus
Hystrix brachyura(= hodgsoni)

Hystrix javanicus
(= yunnanensis)

Atherurus macrourus
Asiatic brush-tailed porcupine

Brief description Small sized animal, weigh 2 – 4 kg. The tail is relatively long, exceeding 20 cm in length. At the end of the tail there are long and hard hollow hairs. The back spine are flattened, between the spine there are long hairs. Inhabits dense forests. Live in burrows dug by them. Feeding habits similar to short tailed porcupine.

Distribution Yunnan, Guizhou, Guangxi and Hainan.

Hystrix brachyra
Malayan short-tailed porcupine

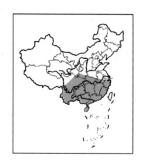

Description Head and body 55 – 77 cm, tail 8 – 14 cm and weight 9.5 – 14 kg. The body is covered with round, hard, and hollowed spines. The spines are shorter on the front of the body, while the spines on the rump can reach a length of 20 – 30 cm. Under the spines there are sparse soft hair. The spines at the end of the tail have specialized into rattle quills.

Habits Inhabits mountain forests, grassland slops at forest edge, and semi – exploited of tropical and subtropical montane slops. The porcupines are nocturnal and terrestrial. They shelter in burrows which they dig themselves and family groups share a burrow system. When moving about the spines makes noise and when in danger, such as encountering an enemy, the porcupine erects the spines on its back and tail, vibrating them with a distinct rattling sound to protect themselves. Feeds on root tubers, root, stems and fruits.

Reproduction Mating occurs from October to November. Gestation lasts about 4 months, female gives birth once a year to 1 – 4 young in spring,

Hystrix brachyura

Tail of the porcupine showing the rattles quills

Myocastoridae

This single genus and species is native to South America. The animals were introduced into China in 1956 from the former Soviet Union for its highly prized pelt. Captive breeding and rearing farms were established throughout the country. But it was a failure due to low economic benefit. In 1990 it was introduced the second time and was again a failure. However, some animals escaped from captivity or when the farms were closed deliberately released. Feral nutrias are found occasionally.

Myocastor coypu Nutria

Description Head and body 43 – 64 cm, tail 26 – 43 cm, and weight 7 – 10 kg. The body is stocky and the head is relatively large. The eyes and ears are small. The snout is short. The hind feet are webbed. The tail is round, covered with scales and sparse short hair.

Habits Inhabits marshes, lakes, and rivers where there are abundant of aquatic plants and trees. The nutrias are semi aquatic rodents, most active in the morning and evening. Feeds on aquatic plants, weeds, wild herds and even twigs of trees and mollusks.

Reproduction Breeding occurs throughout the year. The females produce 2 or more litters a year or 5 litters in 2 years. The estrous cycle is 25 – 27 days. Gestation lasts about 133 days and are able to mate 3 days after labor. Litter size 5 – 7 young, up to 11 – 12 young. Sexual maturity in 5 months. Life span is 5 – 6 year.

Distribution Originally from South America, but by the 30' they were introduced into many countries to establish captive breeding farms.

Myocastor coypu

LAGOMORPHA

Lagomorpha vary from the size of a pika or a rat to that of large hares and rabbits. The body weight of lagomorpha range from 2 – 3 kg. The lagomorpha all have well developed incisors that grow throughout life. Canines are absent. All have an empty space between the incisor and the chin teeth which resembles rodentia, but lagomorpha have 2 pairs of upper incisors and the second pair of incisors being smaller and it is directly behind the first pair of incisors which is different from rodents. The lower jaw has 1 pair of incisors. Lagomorpha are tailless or have short tail. The upper lip has a naked longitudinal groove. Feeds on green vegetation. The lagomorpha are widely distributed in Asia, Europe, Africa and America. There are 72 species in families of Ochotonidae and Leparidae. China has 2 families and 29 species.

Ochotonidae	20	species
Leporidae	9	species

Ochotonidae

Rat sized, herbivorous animals. Head and body length only 12 – 25 cm, and weighs less than 400 g. There is no tail, or very short covered by fur and not visible. The ears are short and rounded with a length of not longer than 4 cm, which is different from rabbits There are only 1 genus with 26 species, of these China has 20 species as follow:

Ochotona alpina	Ochotona iliensis
* Ochotona cansus	Ochotona koslowi
* Ochotona curzoniae	Ochotona ladacensis
* Ochotona daurica	* Ochotona macrotis
Ochotona erythrotis	Ochotona muliensis
Ochotona forresti	Ochotona nubrica
Ochotona gaoligongensis	Ochotona pallasii
Ochotona gloveri	Ochotona roylei
Ochotona himalayana	Ochotona thibetana
Ochotona huangensis	Ochotona thomasi

LAGOMORPHA

Ochotona daurica Daurian pika

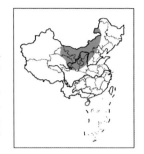

Description Head and body 12.5 – 19 cm, tail 1.5 – 2.2 cm, and weight 110 – 150 g. The body is yellowish brown with some black hair mixed in.

Habits Inhabits sandy and semi sandy steppes below altitudes of 3000m, and dry cultivated areas. It is a ground dwelling species. It lives in colonies, active mostly by day. Feeds on roots, stems and seeds. It does not hibernate, but starts to store food in September for winter use.

Reproduction Mating occurs from May to September. Produce 2 or 3 litters per year. The gestation period is around 30 days, and gives birth to 3 – 7 young, which are sexual maturity in 3 months.

Distribution Nei Mongol, and Gansu.

Ochotona curzoniae Black-lipped pika

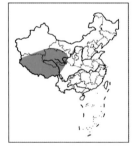

Description Head and body 14 – 19 cm, ears is 1.8 – 2.6 cm, and weight 130 – 195 g. Resembles the Daurian pika, but the edge of the upper and lower lips are black brown. The back is brownish yellow or sandy yellowish brown above and the belly pale yellow or sandy yellowish brown.

Habits Inhabits alpine steppes, and meadow zones at altitudes of 3200 – 5200m. They are active both day and night, lives in colonies. Feeds on leguminous and herbaceous plants. Do not hibernate.

Reproduction Mating occurs from April to September. Usually 2 – 3 litters in a year. Litter size 1 – 8 young, usually 3 – 6 young.

Distribution Qingzang plateau.

Ochotona daurica

Ochotoma curzoniae

LAGOMORPHA

Ochotona cansus Kansu pika

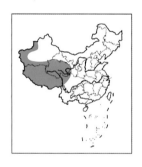

Description Head and body 10.7 – 16.2 cm, tail 2 cm, weight 51 – 82 g. The ears are black with white edges. In summer the back is dull yellowish brown and in winter is grayish yellow brown and the belly pure white.

Habits Inhabits alpine meadows, steppes and shrublands at altitudes of 2300 – 4000 m. They are ground dwelling animals, active mostly at day. Feeds on moss and herbaceous plants. They do not hibernate.

Reproduction Mating occurs from May throughout September. The gestation period is about 30 days, there are 2 litters in a year each with 2 – 6 young. The young reach adult weight in about 40 – 50 days. The longevity is about 5 years.

Distribution Gansu, Qinghai and Sichuan.

Ochotona macrotis Large eared pika

Description Head and body 15.7 – 20 cm, ears about 3 cm, weight 120 – 200 g. The back of the ears are pale brown and inner-sides grayish white with dense long hair. The coat is pale grayish brown on the back or pale brownish yellow, the belly is white.

Habits Inhabits high rocky areas. It is solitary and active at day. Found in crevices of rocks, stone and ice. It does not hibernate, but store food winter use.

Reproduction Mating occurs in spring. Annually produce 1 – 3 litters, the litter size is 1 – 7 young. The young are sexual maturity the following year.

Distribution Qingzang plateau.

Ochotona cansus

Ochotona macrotis

281

LAGOMORPHA

Leporidae

Members of this family are relatively large. Head and body length is 30 – 45 cm, weigh 1.4 – 7 kg. The tail is short with a length of 4 – 10 cm. The ears are long and narrow, usually 6 – 9 cm in length. The proximal part of the ear is tubular. There are 11 genera and 46 species. Of these 1 genus and 46 species are distributed in China.

* *Lepus capensis*
* *Lepus comus*
  Lepus hainanus
  Lepus mandschurius
  Lepus melainus

* *Lepus oiostolus*
  Lepus sinensis
  Lepus timidus
* *Lepus yarkandensis*

Lepus timidus Arctic hare

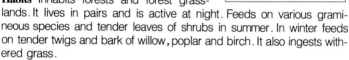

Description Head and body 45 – 54 cm, tail 5 – 5.7 cm, ears 8 – 11 cm, and weight 1.8 – 2.7 kg. In summer the pelage is tawny brown, and the ear tips black. In winter the entire pelage is white but the ear tips remain black. The middle part of the tail is pale brown while the underparts and sides are white.

Habits Inhabits forests and forest grasslands. It lives in pairs and is active at night. Feeds on various gramineous species and tender leaves of shrubs in summer. In winter feeds on tender twigs and bark of willow, poplar and birch. It also ingests withered grass.

Reproduction Mating occurs in spring. Gestation lasts 47 – 55 days. Females produce 2 litters annually, with to 4 – 6 young, maximum 10 per litter. The young are born with their eyes open and are able to move and crawl around. Longevity is 7 years.

Distribution Nei Mongol, Heilongjiang, and northern Xinjiang.

Conservation China: II.

Lepus timidus (winter coat)

Lepus timidus (summer coat)

LAGOMORPHA

Lepus comus Yunnan hare

Description Head and body 41 – 50 cm, tail 7 – 8 cm, ear 10 – 14 cm, and weight 18 – 2.2 kg. The ears are especially long. The dorsal side of the pelage is black brown, with mixture of light brownish yellow fur. The central portion of the tail is grayish black and the underside grayish white.

Habits Inhabits alpine meadows, and steppes areas, it prefers bunchgrass, bunchshrubs, hilly lands and ravines. It is also found in forest fringes and in sparse forests. It is nocturnal. Feeds on forbs and tender leaves of shrubs. It also infests young wheat, cornfields and bean crops.

Reproduction Mating last from April to October. The females produce 2 litters annually, each with 1 – 4 young.

Distribution Yunnan, western Quizhou and southern Sichuan.

Lepus capnesis Cape hare

Description Head and body 38 – 48 cm, tail 9 – 10 cm, ear 8 – 12 cm, and weight 2 – 3 kg. The upper part is yellowish brown, ear tips dull brown. The back of the tail is blackish brown and under part and sides are white.

Habits Inhabits forest slops, cultivated lands, semi-desert, oasis, sand dunes and bunchshrubs. Active both day and night. Feeds mainly on herbaceous vegetation as well as potato leaves, seedlings of wheat and leguminous.

Reproduction Mating occurs in late winter in southern China. Births take place in spring. Gestation lasts about 42 days, produce 2 – 4 litters in a year each litter has 2 – 6 young. The young that are born in early spring are sexual maturity in late summer.

Distribution North of Yangzi River.

Lepus comus

Lepus capensis

LAGOMORPHA

Lepus oiostolus Woolly hare

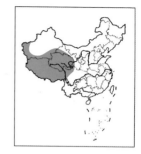

Description Head and body 35 – 56 cm, tail 7 – 12 cm, ear about 12 cm, and weight about 3 kg. The pelage is long and bushy, grayish yellow on the back. The ears dark color. The back of the tail is dull gray, and the underside and sides white.

Habits Inhabits rocky areas of cold steppes, meadows, bunchshrubs, hilly land and forest fringes at altitudes of 2700 – 5200 m. It is active both day and night, but most active in the morning and evening. Feeds mainly on a wide variety of plants, including leaves and stems of small shrubs.

Reproduction Mating occurs in spring. Pregnant females are seen in April. Annually produces 2 litters, each with 4 – 6 young.

Distribution Qingzang plateau.

Lepus yarkandensis Yankand hare

Description Head and body 35 – 43 cm, tail 5 – 9 cm, ear 9 – 11 cm, and weight 1.4 – 1.6 kg. The coat is thick and dense, sandy brown on the back, mixed with fine grayish black stripes. The body sides sandy yellow and the underside white. The tail back has grayish brown stripes.

Habits Inhabits a variety of desert environments and oasis of Talimu basin. Most active in the morning and evening in growths of red osier and in short xeric reeds. In the daytime rests under shrubs. Feeds on tender stems of reeds and a variety leaves and thin twigs of shrubs.

Reproduction Mating occurs in April and August. Produces 2 – 3 litters a year, each with 3 – 5 young.

Distribution An endemic species of China. Distributed in Talimu basin and adjacent areas in Xingjiang.

Lepus oiostolus

Lepus yarkandensis

SELECT BIBLIOGRAPHY

马逸清等著. 1986. 黑龙江省兽类志. 哈尔滨: 黑龙江科学技术出版社

王岐山主编. 1990. 安徽兽类志. 合肥: 安徽科学技术出版社

王香亭主编. 1990. 宁夏脊椎动物志. 银川: 宁夏人民出版社

王香亭主编. 1991. 甘肃脊椎动物志. 兰州: 甘肃科学技术出版社

冯祚建, 蔡桂全, 郑昌琳. 1986. 西藏哺乳类. 北京: 科学出版社

西北高原研究所. 1989. 青海经济动物志. 西宁: 青海人民出版社

陈万青编. 1978. 海兽检索手册. 北京: 科学出版社

张荣祖等著. 1997. 中国哺乳动物分布. 北京: 中国林业出版社

罗泽珣著. 1988. 中国野兔. 北京: 中国林业出版社

袁国映主编. 1991. 新疆脊椎动物简志. 乌鲁木齐: 新疆人民出版社

罗蓉等编著. 1993. 贵州兽类志. 贵阳: 贵州科技出版社

胡锦矗, 王酉之主编. 1984. 四川资源动物志. 成都: 四川科学技术出版社

诸葛阳等主编. 1989. 浙江动物志——兽类. 杭州: 浙江科学技术出版

高耀亭等编著. 1987. 中国动物志——食肉类. 北京: 科学出版社

盛和林等编. 1994. 毛皮动物手册. 上海: 上海辞书出版社

盛和林等著. 1992. 中国鹿类动物. 上海: 华东师范大学出版社

褚新洛主编. 1989. 云南省卷六——动物志. 昆明: 云南人民出版社

Corbet, G. B. & Hill, J. E. 1991. A world list of mammalian species London: British Museum (Natural History)

Corbet, G. B. & Hill, J. E. 1992 The mammals of the Indomalayan Region: A systematic review. British Museum (Naturai History)

Index of Latin Names

289

Index of Latin Names

Index of Latin Names

Index of English Names

Index of English Names

Sheng Helin: Professor of Mammalogy at the East China Normal University and Director of the Zoological Ecology Research Program. He has been involved in the field of animal ecology and mammalogy for over 40 years, as a researcher of the field and as a teacher. In the late 20 years, he has devoted himself entirely to deer studies in China. His representative publications are An Introduction to Mammalogy, Manual of Fur – bearing Animals and the Deer in China. He is currently Deputy Editor in Chief of Acta Theriologica Sinica and Wildlife, and Vice Chairman of China Mammal Society and member of Deer Specialists Group of the Species survival Commission I-UCN.

Noriyuku Ohtaishi: Professor of Mammalogy in the Department of Veterinary, Hokkaido University. He has been conducting researches and teaching on the Mammalogy, Comparative Anatomy, Zoological Classification, Systemic Evolution and Zoological Geography for more than 35 years. Since 1986, Professor Ohtaishi has conducting a series of research on the deer in the Qinghai – Tibetan Plateau, Northeastern China, and Xinjiang.

Lu Houji: Professor of Ecology and Director of the Centre for Conservation Biology at the East China Normal University. He has conducted Conservation Biology and Wildlife Management Training Courses in China with the Smithsonian Institution since 1987. Recent interests in research are the Conservation Biology, the Behavioral Ecology and the Mammalian Ecology.